Engaging and Empowering Aboriginal Youth:
A toolkit for service providers

Claire V. Crooks, Ph.D., C.Psych.
CAMH Centre for Prevention Science
and The University of Western Ontario

Debbie Chiodo, M.A., M.Ed.
CAMH Centre for Prevention Science
and The University of Western Ontario

Darren Thomas, BSc.
New Orators Youth Project
and Wilfrid Laurier University

Order this book online at www.trafford.com/09-0178
or email orders@trafford.com

Most Trafford titles are also available at major online book retailers.

Note for Librarians: A cataloguing record for this book is available from Library
and Archives Canada at www.collectionscanada.ca/amicus/index-e.html

Production of this document has been made possible through a financial contribution from the Public Health Agency of Canada.
The views expressed herein do not necessarily represent the views of the Public Health Agency Canada.

Most of the quotes used in this manual have been provided by partners and colleagues in written or verbal communication to the
first author. In all cases authors have approved the final quotes.

Quotes not obtained in this manner include the quotes from Chief Luther Standing Bear and Chief Dan George (pages 58 and 65
respectively), which were accessed online at the First People: Words of Wisdom site: http://www.firstpeople.us/FP-Html-Wisdom/
wisdom.html. The quote from the AHF Regional Gathering participant on page 10 is from the Spring 2001 issue of Healing Words,
a publication of the AHF available at http://www.ahf.ca/pages/download/28_54. The quote from Roberta Jamieson on page 398
was taken from the website Famous Canadian Women at http://famouscanadianwomen.com/quotes/quotes%20page.htm. Finally,
the quote from Dr. Peter Menzies was excerpted from his publication, Longing to return home: From intergenerational trauma to
intergenerational healing in the CAMH journal, Cross Currents: The Journal of Addiction and Mental Health.

Printed in Victoria, BC, Canada.

ISBN: 978-1-4269-0429-5

www.trafford.com

North America & international
toll-free: 1 888 232 4444 (USA & Canada)
phone: 250 383 6864 ✦ fax: 250 383 6804
email: info@trafford.com

The United Kingdom & Europe
phone: +44 (0)1865 487 395 ✦ local rate: 0845 230 9601
facsimile: +44 (0)1865 481 507 ✦ email: info.uk@trafford.com

10 9 8 7 6 5 4 3 2

PREFACE

How do you make programs more appropriate and relevant for Aboriginal youth? This toolkit grew out of conversations that a number of us in the field of violence prevention and youth programming have had about this topic. We were all in agreement that programs cannot be one-size-fits-all, and that most mainstream programs do not adequately match the unique needs and strengths of Aboriginal youth. However, there was little agreement about *how* to undertake this process. Furthermore, we were unable to find literature to guide us in the adaptation process.

This toolkit is our attempt to provide such a guide for front-line service providers, facilitators, educators, community partners and researchers. We hope that individuals from all of these groups will find something in this manual to help them improve their work with Aboriginal youth.

The first two authors of this toolkit are non-Aboriginal researchers and clinicians trained in health promotion, quantitative research, program development and evaluation. We work at the CAMH Centre for Prevention Science in London, Ontario. Through our work at the Centre (along with colleagues David Wolfe, Peter Jaffe, and Ray Hughes) we have developed a range of school-based violence prevention initiatives for both Aboriginal and non-Aboriginal youth. We are involved with several national research and community partner networks, most notably PREVNet and the Canadian Prevention Science Cluster. The third author, Darren Thomas, is a Motivational Consultant and Community Educator from Six Nations of the Grand River. He is Seneca Bear clan of the Haudenosaunee and has worked with communities across the country in a number of consulting capacities. He developed the New Orators Youth Project in his home community to foster mentoring and public education opportunties. Collectively the authors have a wide range of experience in research, program development, and working with youth and community partners. More information about the authors is provided in Appendix A.

In 2005 we received a three-year grant from the Public Health Agency of Canada's Population Health Fund to investigate the process of adapting programs for Aboriginal youth. We received this grant through partnerships with the BC/Yukon Society for Transition Houses in Vancouver and New Directions for Children, Youth, Adults and Families in Winnipeg. Although each of the sites undertakes very different types of youth programming, the idea was for each to document the process they had embarked on with respect to adapting their programs. The documentation part was critical, because so much of the wisdom and guidance in this area was being shared verbally. A careful documentation process would allow us to identify common themes across sites that might serve as principles and strategies for adapting programs. In some cases, the documentation process would serve to capture excellent culturally-relevant services that were already in place. Brief descriptions of the core sites for this project are included in Appendix B.

This toolkit has grown far beyond the lessons learned from the project mentioned above. It has also grown far beyond the scope of violence prevention to encompass youth programming in general. Earlier versions of this book were sent to a wide range of reviewers, and in many cases these reviewers contributed through the provision of additional case studies and suggestions for additional considerations. In some cases reviewers connected the authors to other individuals who also became contributors. Contributors and toolkit reviewers are listed in Appendices C and D.

ACKNOWLEDGEMENTS

The work represented in this guide is based on wisdom and experience generously shared by many individuals and groups. From the outset we received invaluable guidance with the proposal from Cindy Blackstock (Executive Director of the *First Nations Child and Family Caring Society*), and Jocelyn Formsma and Ginger Gosnell (Youth Consultants). We thank our original partner sites – the *BC/Yukon Society of Transition Houses (BCYSTH)* and *New Directions for Children, Youth, Adults and Families (ND)* – with whom we obtained funding for this project.

In British Columbia the *BCYSTH* joined with *Helping Spirit Lodge, Nuxalk Nation,* the *Vancouver School Board (VSB),* the *School Age Children and Youth, Substance Use Prevention Initiative (SACY),* and the *Urban Native Youth Association,* each of whom provided valuable partnerships and experiences. In Ontario, the *Fourth R* partnered with the *Thames Valley District School Board,* a partnership which has been integral to the success of their school-based initiatives. The Fourth R has also benefitted immeasurably from the wisdom, humour, and patience of Darren Thomas, founder of the *New Orators Youth Project* from Six Nations. All of the sites have learned from other local and provincial partners, too numerous to name, and the contributions of all of these people have shaped this document.

We appreciate the assistance of those individuals who provided comments and feedback on earlier drafts of this toolkit. Collectively, they are leaders in Aboriginal health issues, programming with youth, research, and applied policy work, and we are exceptionally grateful for their time and assistance. The toolkit was strengthened immeasurably by these reviewers alerting the authors to other exceptional resources, or in many cases, writing additional sections and case studies themselves. We have tried to acknowledge contributors who wrote particular sections throughout the document.

We gratefully acknowledge Shanna Burns, CAMH Centre for Prevention Science Research Associate, for her skillful assistance in designing the lay-out of this toolkit. We also thank Mary Jane Crooks for her careful review of the final proofs.

We are indebted to the financial support provided by the Public Health Agency of Canada (PHAC) through their Population Health Fund. We appreciate the hands-on guidance and feedback from the Policy Analysts (first David Allen, then Salena Brickey) throughout the course of the project, as well as the oversight from Yvonne Côté. Beyond funding the initial project, PHAC has generously provided additional funds for the printing and distribution of the toolkit, as well as a French translation.

Finally, we thank all of the youth involved with the projects and organizations who contributed to this toolkit. Their energy, wisdom, and strength are an inspiration to all of us.

Claire Crooks and Debbie Chiodo, Project Co-Leads

TABLE OF CONTENTS

SECTION 1: Background and Overview

OVERVIEW: THE CASE FOR STRENGTH-BASED PROGRAMMING

Not a week goes by without a negative news story about the rates of problem behaviours among Aboriginal youth in Canada. Violence, substance use, suicide, gangs… rates of these behaviours are higher among Aboriginal youth than their non-Aboriginal peers. However, these statistics do not tell the whole story. Rather than focusing on these negative statistics, we must shift our whole paradigm of intervention to a strengths-based approach. A strengths-based approach focuses on developing assets that are known protective factors, such as strong relationships, life skills, and school connectedness.

WHY DO WE NEED PROGRAMS AT ALL?

> *"It's where our parents are coming from. It's where our grandparents are coming from. By the time you get to my generation, we have all the baggage and we don't know where it comes from."*
> Kristen Hendrick, Elected Councillor, Chippewas on the Thames

A strengths-based approach is critical for Aboriginal youth because it takes the Canadian historical context into account. By placing the high rates of violence, substance abuse, and poverty experienced by Aboriginal families into the context of colonization and assimilation, this perspective shifts the perceived deficits away from the individual and allows us to focus instead on the resilience many of these youth have demonstrated. Within this broader context of colonization and assimilation, it can be seen that the deliberate suppression and elimination of culture has left a legacy of intergenerational trauma. Although it is difficult to quantify direct effects, the long history of cultural oppression and marginalization has contributed to high levels of social, emotional, spiritual and mental health problems in many Aboriginal communities. This history continues to affect Aboriginal people today through the racism and discrimination that they face. These challenges are compounded by higher rates of poverty and substandard housing.

Knowledge production is another important element of our shared post-colonial history. Simply put, colonization has everything to do with who gets to define reality and write the textbooks! As a result, indigenous knowledge and worldviews are absent from mainstream education and dialogue. When they are presented, these views tend to be relegated to a less valuable position. There is a significant need to find ways for mainstream organizations to integrate cultural wisdom and views into their programs.

> *"Intergenerational trauma requires the counsellor to review the person symptomatically from a historical perspective. We need to consider the individual as a member of both an extended family and a community, with a distinct social and political history."*
> Dr. Peter Menzies (2006, p.12)
> Manager Aboriginal Services, CAMH

For youth, lack of connection to culture has been identified as a clear risk factor in respect to violence. Thus, promoting youth assets within a framework that emphasizes cultural connection is a good fit for Aboriginal youth. Shifting from seeing youth 'at risk' to 'at promise' requires a fundamental shift in how we approach programming. It requires promoting strong youth within a holistic framework, rather than targeting single risk or problem behaviors in isolation.

What is the Role of Non-Aboriginal Individuals and Organizations?

Given the historical context in which we are working, many people have legitimate questions about the role of non-Aboriginal individuals and organizations. How do mainstream organizations help support Aboriginal youth, families, and communities, without further entrenching the existing power structures? We think the answer to that lies in how the work is approached. When youth are approached from a place of respect, a place that recognizes historical context, and a place of partnership, then this work can be achieved in a way that honours all of the participants. Furthermore, within our shared history of colonization and assimilation, there is an obligation of the part of individuals and organizations in the dominant culture to find ways to balance out historical wrongs by helping to bring wider recognition to the immense value of indigenous knowledge and ways of practice.

Our Four Guiding Principles of Enhanced Programming

Although the initial focus of our project was on adapting specific programs and program materials, we have come to realize that working effectively with Aboriginal youth requires a unique approach. Changing manuals and program materials is only one small step of the process. Based on our understanding of the hallmarks of effective programs, and in consultation with existing literature and policy reports, we have identified four guiding principles for successfully working with Aboriginal youth. The extensive review process that we undertook in developing this toolkit reassured us of the validity of these principles, as our reviewers confirmed that these principles matched their own observations about effective programs.

Guiding Principles for Successful Programming

1. Understanding and integrating cultural identity

2. Increasing youth engagement

3. Fostering youth empowerment

4. Establishing and maintaining effective partnerships

This toolkit represents an attempt to pull together some of our lessons to help guide other individuals and organizations who want to follow their own paths to adaptation and enhancement of their programs.

The first section offers some ***introductory materials*** to provide context for working with Aboriginal youth. Although this toolkit addresses issues much broader than violence prevention, we have included information about violence prevention and what is known about culturally-specific protective factors as a framework.

In the second section we describe ***specific strategies***. We have organized our considerations and strategies around the four key principles of enhancement that we identified. In each section we have attempted to provide some balance between broad guidelines and specific strategies.

The third section is devoted to ***working with schools***. All of our partners are engaged with the educational system in some manner, and we have all found that the uniqueness of the education system requires particular strategies.

In the fourth section we address ***research issues***. This section includes information for organizations undertaking self-assessment and program evaluation, as well as information for Aboriginal and non-Aboriginal academic and community-based researchers.

We have interspersed several case examples throughout the toolkit that demonstrate the application of our guiding principles. Contact information for the organizations described in the case studies is available in Appendix E. We have also provided the glossary from the Reconciliation Movement website (www.reconciliationmovement.org) and a list of acronyms to assist readers (Appendices F and G respectively).

For the non-Aboriginal members of this project, these are the lessons we wish we had known at the outset of our work and the ways in which our awareness has developed over time. Clearly this is an ongoing process and we imagine that we will update this toolkit. For the Aboriginal members of the project, these are lessons we have shared and think would assist other organizations. For all of us, these are the principles and experiences that we identify as fundamental to our successful partnerships and programs.

In conducting our work in this area, we encountered some resources that were helpful to us, particularly those created by Aboriginal organizations. We have included some of these resources in this toolkit in the hope that others may find them similarly helpful. This borrowing of resources and templates has been done with appropriate permission and acknowledgement.

THERE ARE A FEW CONSIDERATIONS THAT REQUIRE COMMENT:

First, we have **used the term Aboriginal with the knowledge that there is not a consensus about whether or not it is an appropriate term**. Some of our partners like the term because it is inclusive (of First Nations, Métis, and Inuit groups). Others do not like the term because it was imposed by others, and suggests a homogeneity that does not exist. We acknowledge that there is a movement across the country for Indigenous Peoples to reclaim their original names in their own languages and recognize that this is an important step towards empowerment and a step closer to decolonization. At the same time, we have chosen to use the term Aboriginal in this document because we feel that the general principles and strategies are useful regardless of which communities are involved. We use this term with respect for individual preference in language and with recognition that there is no one Aboriginal culture or set of traditions. We also offer some guidelines and suggestions with respect to language and terminology, as we know this is a daunting area for many service providers.

Second, **some readers may find parts of this toolkit overly elementary and obvious and others may find some of the strategies impossible to weave into their own work at this time**. We recognize that there is a continuum in terms of how far along people are in providing culturally relevant and empowering programming for Aboriginal youth. Our goal in writing this toolkit was to have something for everyone such that those beginning this process can find simple starting strategies and those who have been working closely with community partners to provide culturally relevant programming can find suggestions to further their success.

Third, we are clear about the **limitations of program-based services for Aboriginal youth and recognize that true healing and empowerment will come from the communities themselves.** As much as programs can do, there are significant underlying structural and socioeconomic issues that need to be addressed. At the same time, our mainstream programs are encountering Aboriginal youth, whether we are located in schools, community agencies, or treatment settings, and we need to improve the quality and cultural appropriateness of our services with these youth.

Fourth, the **Aboriginal community is broad and diverse.** Just as there are the First Nations, Métis, and Inuit, there are also the urban, rural, on-Reserve and off-Reserve. Each individual young person, parent, program participant, social worker, program coordinator or teacher will have varying levels of belief and understanding of their own culture as well as other Aboriginal cultures.

Finally, one of the most important lessons we learned over the course of this project is that **a cookie-cutter approach to enhancing services for Aboriginal youth will never succeed.** The path an organization travels will depend on the population of youth with whom they work, their pre-existing relationships with community members, and their particular mandate. We offer the strategies and lessons in this guide as possible starting points for others wishing to enhance the quality of the services they are providing to Aboriginal youth, but recognize that each organization will need to find their own path with their partners.

THE PREVENTION / HEALTH PROMOTION SPECTRUM

Different types of prevention and health promotion activities exist along a spectrum. These different approaches differ in terms of the extent to which the youth involved are already experiencing significant challenges, and the focus of activities.

Tertiary Prevention | Secondary Prevention | Universal Prevention | Health Promotion

HEALTH PROMOTION

The Canadian Red Cross *Walking the Prevention Circle* program (see case study starting on page 18) takes a health promotion approach by engaging all members of the community in a dialogue and naming and understanding violence within an historical context. It builds on the strengths of community leaders and provides opportunities for those struggling with violence and other issues to become part of the community solution.

PRIMARY PREVENTION

Primary prevention initiatives focus on targeting factors that might potentially cause difficulties among all Aboriginal youth, regardless of whether individuals are showing any signs of difficulty. *The Fourth R: Uniting Our Nations* (see case study starting on page 74) classroom-based curricula that address violence, substance use, and unsafe sexual behavior are examples of primary prevention.

SECONDARY PREVENTION

By developing and delivering services for Aboriginal youth who have been exposed to domestic violence, the BCYSTH approaches violence prevention at the secondary prevention level. Through the VIP program (see case study starting on page 78) they deliver service to youth who are at increased risk for violence on the basis of their family history, but who may not be exhibiting violence at the present time.

TERTIARY PREVENTION (TREATMENT)

The *Transition and Education Resources for Females (TERF)* program (see case study starting on page 30) at *New Directions* provides tertiary prevention through its focus on youth who have already been victimized by their involvement in the sex trade. At TERF, prevention is conceptualized as meeting youths' most basic needs and helping them to get off the street and develop skills for alternative careers. By achieving these goals, youth are at lower risk for experiencing violence by virtue of providing them with a safer environment.

UNIVERSAL VERSUS CULTURALLY SPECIFIC RISK AND PROTECTIVE FACTORS ASSOCIATED WITH VIOLENCE

Risk factors raise the likelihood of a negative outcome for an individual and protective factors reduce this likelihood. There are some risk and protective factors that appear to work the same way across cultures.[1] These universal factors are important to address in any prevention program. Others protective factors may be culturally specific, or, particular protective factors may have culturally-specific relevance.

UNIVERSAL FACTORS RELATED TO VIOLENCE

Risk Factors	Protective Factors	Culturally Specific Protective Factors
• Deep poverty • Poor mental health • Drug and alcohol abuse	• Strong families • Appropriate discipline • Academic achievement	• Traditional culture and values, including spirituality • Access to community Elders • Increased cultural emphasis on specific protective factors - such as healthy families and strong community networks

Given the overlap of risk and protective factors across cultures, it is not necessary to throw out everything we have learned about effective prevention programming with non-Aboriginal youth. Rather, the challenge is to incorporate this awareness of culturally-specific protective factors into existing practices.

---

[1] For an excellent review of risk and protective factors for delinquency among Native Americans, see Pridemore, W. A. (2004). Review of the literature of risk and protective factors of offending among Native Americans. Although written based on research in the United States, it makes a sound argument equally applicable in the Canadian context.

Engaging and Empowering Aboriginal Youth: A Toolkit for Service Providers

GENERAL BEST PRACTICE VIOLENCE PREVENTION PRINCIPLES

Successful prevention programs tend to share a number of features. Although not all programs can achieve all of these goals, they are an important starting place for thinking about best practice violence prevention programming. Research tells us that the most effective approaches are[2]:

Holistic

- Effective programs target multiple levels of influence, such as individuals, parents, school climate, and teacher training. They can also be comprehensive with respect to addressing overlapping risk behaviors. By definition a comprehensive approach suggests a reasonable duration, and cannot be achieved through single activities, such as a guest speaker or assembly alone.

Skill-based

- Communication and problem-solving skills are taught in effective programs. These programs use interactive, skill-based strategies (such as role play), and do not rely solely on information and lecturing approaches to transfer skills. Life skills training is considered an effective intervention across cultural groups, particularly for individuals who face multiple risk factors.

Pick appropriate targets

- Effective programs focus on factors known to be related to the problem behavior. Attitudes and skills, school connectedness, and coping skills are examples of appropriate prevention targets because they are all implicated in the development and use of violence. Bystander involvement is another excellent target because of the role played by bystanders in violence (particularly bullying).

Engage peers

- Effective programs may include peer facilitators, a peer mentoring component or youth committee. The use of peers is important because youth identify more readily with these role models.

Include parents and guardians

- Although the extent and nature of appropriate parental involvement depends on the age of the youth, parental involvement is regarded as a critical component for effective prevention programs.

Change the larger environment

- Effective programs recognize the complex ecology of youths' lives and work to change these environments. For example, school-based programming may attempt to alter norms about help-seeking, and build the capacity of educators to respond to violence, thus altering the school environment.

---

[2] See Wolfe, D. A., Jaffe, P.G., & Crooks, C. V. (2006). *Adolescent risk behaviors: Why teens experiment and strategies to keep them safe.* New Haven, CT: Yale University Press.

PRINCIPLES FOR SUCCESSFUL PROGRAMMING FOR ABORIGINAL YOUTH

Based on the work of the groups involved with this project, lessons learned from other organizations and researchers, and a review of existing research and policy literature, we identified four major principles for enhancing youth programs. These principles supplement the best practice principles that apply more generally and are described in the following section.

UNDERSTANDING AND INTEGRATING CULTURAL IDENTITY

The loss of cultural identity and values is a major risk factor faced by Aboriginal youth. It is critical to address this loss in programming for youth.

INCREASING YOUTH ENGAGEMENT

Youth engagement is both a process and a desired outcome. Youth engagement means providing a range of roles for youth who become involved and providing them with opportunities to become leaders in addition to participants.

Principles

FOSTERING YOUTH EMPOWERMENT

Empowerment is an extension of youth engagement. Empowerment includes supporting youth in the development of skills, competence and identity, but also supporting them in using these skills for social change.

ESTABLISHING AND MAINTAINING EFFECTIVE PARTNERSHIPS

Effective and appropriate partnerships are an important foundation to any prevention programming, but the importance of these relationships is amplified when working with Aboriginal youth and their communities.

OVERVIEW OF PRINCIPLES

Subsequent sections of this toolkit address the guiding principles in detail and provide specific strategies for applying these principles. A brief overview of the principles is offered below.

Principle 1: Understanding and Integrating Cultural Identity

- Substance use and suicide prevention research has shown that strength of cultural identity can be a powerful protective factor for youth.
- Bicultural competence is an important idea related to cultural identity in that youth who have the skills, values and attitudes necessary to be successful in their traditional community as well as in the dominant culture will be better able to make positive and healthy choices in a range of areas.

Principle 2: Increasing Youth Engagement

- Youth who are engaged with prosocial activities, their schools, and their communities exhibit fewer risk behaviours than peers who are not connected.
- Youth who are engaged culturally participate in cultural activities or can access these in their communities. Cultural engagement is an important protective factor against a range of negative outcomes.

Principle 3: Fostering Youth Empowerment

- There are two types of empowerment that are important for youth, particularly those who belong to a culture that has been marginalized.
- Personal empowerment, stems from individual youth having the necessary skills and opportunities to meet personal goals and develop into well-adjusted adults. Social empowerment, refers to having power to positively change the environment through work with the community, school, or larger social arenas.
- Targeting youth empowerment requires providing opportunities and support for youth to become agents of social change themselves.

Principle 4: Establishing and Maintaining Effective Partnerships

- Partnerships are important because of the emphasis on extended family and social networks among traditional cultures.
- Partnerships are the source of cultural teachings and priorities, particularly when program developers and evaluators are not from the same communities.
- Partnerships increase buy-in from youth and communities.

SECTION 2: GUIDING PRINCIPLES

Principle 1: Understanding and Integrating Cultural Identity

Principle 2: Increasing Youth Engagement

Principle 3: Fostering Youth Empowerment

Principle 4: Developing and Maintaining Effective Partnerships

PRINCIPLE 1:
UNDERSTANDING AND INTEGRATING CULTURAL IDENTITY

Cultural identity is fundamental to how we see ourselves and the world. The impact of systematic attempts to destroy culture has resulted in many Aboriginal youth, their families and communities, being disconnected from traditional values and teachings. Cultural identity is a complicated area in that it means different things to different people. Aboriginal youth in particular need to reclaim a healthy sense of identity and what it means for them to be Aboriginal living in Canada. In the absence of such an understanding, identity may be equated with rejecting anything seen as part of the dominant culture. Too often that means a rejection of institutions, such as school, that will provide important skills and opportunities for youth in the long run. Thus, incorporating healthy and positive messages about cultural identity is a critical part of providing good service to Aboriginal youth. Culture enhancing activities can help re-connect youth to protective influences from which they have become disengaged, and help them develop a sense of pride in who they are.

> *"When I was growing up, when I was in the residential schools, I was lost for a very long time....I didn't hear the drum beat, I heard the organ. It took me 36 years to find out who I am."*
>
> (AHF Regional Gathering Participant, November 9, 2000)

> *The right of children to know their culture and language is protected by the UN Convention on the Rights of the Child as well as the UN Declaration on the Rights of Indigenous Peoples.*

GOALS OF CULTURE ENHANCING ACTIVITIES

Culture-enhancing activities can serve a number of purposes. The following five goals of cultural enhancement activities are identified by the Centre for Suicide Prevention in their document, *Aboriginal Youth: A Manual of Promising Suicide Prevention Strategies:*[3]

- Share elements of Aboriginal culture and traditions that may have been lost to the new generation.
- Enhance personal resources of youth such as a sense of well-being, belonging, security, identity, and self-esteem.
- Provide youth with alternate options they can rely on when in need.
- Facilitate the development of meaningful relationships between youth and the older generation.
- Help children and youth bridge the gap between Aboriginal culture and its non-Aboriginal counterpart.

---

[3] White, J. and Jodoin, N. (2007). *Aboriginal youth: A manual of promising suicide prevention strategies.* Calgary, AB: Centre for Suicide Prevention. Available online at http://www.suicideinfo.ca/csp/assets/promstrat_manual.pdf

CULTURAL IDENTITY: WHOSE CULTURE?

The term "Aboriginal" does not describe one particular cultural group. It is a legal term, defined in the Constitution, to encompass individuals of First Nations, Métis, and Inuit backgrounds. These groups differ widely from each other in terms of culture, history, language, and beliefs, and to group them together as a cultural entity is misleading. Furthermore, "Aboriginal" is not a term that Indigenous People chose for themselves, and most individuals have more specific and accurate cultural identifiers that prefer. Within the three large groups defined as Aboriginal, there are important distinctions, as each Nation has their own rich culture and history. For example, there are over 600 registered bands in Canada, and at one time there were hundreds of distinct languages, although many of these are now extinct. Today there are approximately 50-60 indigenous languages (belonging to 11 major language families) spoken in Canada[4]. Thirty percent of these remaining languages have been placed on the endangered list.

Keeping this context in mind, we offer the following considerations about cultural identity:

1. Be clear which First Nation, Inuit or Métis community you are enhancing your program for and incorporate the traditions, stories, and teachings of that community.

2. It is not always possible to gear a program to one specific culture, because we are often working with individuals of various cultural backgrounds, particularly in urban settings. In these cases, the following suggestions can be considered:

    a. If you combine traditions and teachings, be clear about where these traditions are coming from (group or individual perspectives). It is disrespectful to mix and match them into one mythical pan-Aboriginal cultural tradition.

    b. There are some traditions that are more universal and will resonate with a wider range of people. For example, the Seven Grandfather Teachings (right) are subscribed to in some form by a range of Aboriginal groups (e.g., Anishinaabe; Seven Virtues among the Cree; also used by the Mi'kmaq). Furthermore, the universality of these values is such that they can be incorporated into a program to benefit all youth.

> ### SEVEN GRANDFATHER TEACHINGS
> 1. *Wisdom*
> 2. *Respect*
> 3. *Love*
> 4. *Bravery*
> 5. *Honesty*
> 6. *Humility*
> 7. *Truth*

---

[4] This figure is taken from the National Resources Canada atlas website and is based on 1996 data. Available at: http://atlas.nrcan.gc.ca/site/english/maps/peopleandsociety/lang/aboriginallanguages/bycommunity. For a more complete report on trends in Aboriginal languages based on 2006 Statistics Canada data see http://www.visions.ab.ca/res/ablangincanada2007.pdf.

LANGUAGE MATTERS

For non-Aboriginal service providers and researchers, the issue of appropriate language can cause stress and anxiety. You may not be sure of the difference between First Nations and Aboriginal and not know who to ask. You may be embarrassed or afraid to say the wrong thing. You may have been told that the word Native is not appropriate, and then at your first meeting with a new community partner, that is how they refer to themselves. You may unknowingly be disrespectful through a lack of knowledge. Use of language is critical, not merely as an issue of "political correctness," but because language is fundamental to people's sense of identity. It is also very rooted in *who* gets to define people or communities. The following considerations and lessons have been shared by Aboriginal partners[5] with the non-Aboriginal members of our team, and provide a starting point:

Some things can be learned from a good glossary.	• Some language issues are factual and can be gleaned from a good reference source. For example, every Canadian should know that there are Reserves in Canada, not Reservations. An excellent glossary is the one found on the Touchstones of Reconciliation website at http://www.reconciliationmovement.org/resources/glossary.html. It is included as Appendix F in this toolkit.
Partnerships provide the best learning opportunities about language.	• While a glossary can define some basic terms, your Aboriginal partners are much more valuable in your learning process. Express an openness to learn and a willingness to be corrected. Listen carefully to terms used by people of the group you are working with so that you can use the same terms. Ask individuals how preference for terminology.
Some terms generally considered outdated have significant legal meanings.	•For example, the term "Indian" is generally considered outdated, but is included in certain foundational legal documents and government ministries. The Indian Act and Indian and Northern Affairs Canada are two examples where this term is still used. Indian status (as defined in the Indian Act) still determines which Aboriginal people are accorded certain rights.
Feeling anxious about terminology and language choices is a natural part of this process.	• Knowing what language to use can be a source of great anxiety for many non-Aboriginal partners. Not wanting to offend other partners or be embarrassed is a natural and predictable reaction to engaging in this work. It is important to remember that these barriers are experienced by most non-Aboriginal individuals at some point in their work. Similar to learning a second language, it is only with practice, feedback and opportunities to learn that you will become more comfortable with terminology.

---

[5] Although these lessons come from conversations with many people, we are particularly grateful for guidance from Cindy Blackstock, Marie Battiste, and Sarah Longman in this regard.

There is a national trend to replace post-colonial tribal names with traditional names.

- Some English language names for specific tribes were based on derogatory terms, bestowed either by English or French speaking colonialists, or other First Nations tribes who were traditional enemies. Many groups have gone through a process of reclaiming their traditional names. For example, the commonly used term, Sioux, is an insult that comes from a French version of an Ojibwa word meaning snakes. The preferred term is Dakota /Nakota / Lakota, which means allies. This reclaiming of traditional names has been an important symbol of empowerment for many communities.

There are regional and individual differences in terminology preferences.

- Just as you would not expect a non-Aboriginal person to represent his or her entire culture with respect to language preferences, it is important to recognize that there are regional and individual differences. Even within a single community there may be differences in the acceptability of specific terms. For example, the use of the term Aboriginal continues to be hotly debated within various organizations. Some like the term because of its inclusivity, while others object to it as overgeneralizing and imposed by non-Aboriginal people. Again, learn from your partners and engage in discussions about the reason for these language debates to better understand the range of viewpoints. As another example, some communities prefer the term Nation to Reserve.

Youth may use terms you have been advised are disrespectful.

- Sometimes when working with youth, they will self-identify with terms that you have been told are disrespectful. These occurrences fall into two categories. The first is when youth use outdated terms like Indian or Native that, for the most part, are being replaced. The manner in which you respond might depend on the situation. For example, in an early encounter or an interview setting, it may be more important to mirror the youth's terminology to build rapport and comfort. In the context of a more well-developed relationship, there might be opportunities to talk about the issue of language and the associated politics. These conversations can help youth become more aware of issues of cultural identity. The second type of situation involves youth using a term (either to describe another youth or themselves) that is clearly derogatory and racialized. In these cases it is important to label the language as harmful and inappropriate.

Language is about more than terminology.

- There are many important issues with respect to language, beyond the choice of single terms. For example, the phrase *Canada's Aboriginal Peoples* denotes a possessive relationship that many Aboriginal people do not recognize. The terms *Aboriginal Peoples of Canada* has the same identification geographically, but without the possessive connotations. Again, your partners are your best teachers for becoming sensitive to these distinctions.

CULTURAL IDENTITY: 10 CONSIDERATIONS AND STRATEGIES

Integrating culture into a program is a process. Similarly, establishing a sense of cultural identity is an ongoing process for the youth and adults involved. The following considerations and strategies are offered as starting points.

1. **AWARENESS OF CULTURAL IDENTITY NEEDS TO BE WOVEN INTO EVERY STEP OF OUR ACTIVITIES.**

Cultural identity is woven through the very fabric of our work. It is not merely a lesson in a curriculum or an activity in a program. It is also about using teachable moments to help youth explore positive and healthy notions of culture and what it means to be a First Nations or Métis or Inuit youth. Incorporation of cultural identity needs to be considered during every step of program development, implementation, delivery, assessment practices, and evaluation.

2. **POSITIVE ROLE MODELS FROM YOUTHS' CULTURAL GROUPS ARE AN INCREDIBLE ASSET IN DEVELOPING A HEALTHY CULTURAL IDENTITY.**

All youth turn to their peers for issues of identity, and this process is amplified among youth who are not part of the dominant culture. Positive peer role models are incredible assets in this regard.

3. **CULTURALLY-RELEVANT TEACHINGS ARE BEST IDENTIFIED THROUGH COMMUNITY PARTNERS.**

Community partners, Cultural Advisors, and Elders are best able to determine the cultural teachings that should be incorporated into a program. Strong and equal relationships with these people provide the foundation for this transfer of knowledge.

4. **CULTURAL IDENTITY NEEDS TO BE REFLECTED IN THE ENVIRONMENT OF THE SETTING.**

All youth need to see themselves reflected in positive ways in the media around them. For example, Aboriginal students need to see posters in the hallways that reflect their heritage. These culturally-diverse posters should not be simply for issues related to culture, but for any positive images (such as work placements, student leaders, etc.).

5. **CULTURAL COMPETENCE NEEDS TO BE FOSTERED AMONG PROFESSIONALS.**

Non-Aboriginal youth and adults working with Aboriginal youth have an obligation to become educated about history, culture, and current events. Program deliverers must be culturally sensitive to effectively respond to the needs of the individual and community. This professional and personal development can include formal activities such as attending conferences, ceremonies, cultural events and reading books, but it is also achieved through informal learning with partners.

6. TRADITIONS AND SYMBOLS ARE IMPORTANT COMPONENTS OF CULTURAL IDENTITY, (BUT THEY ARE NOT THE SUM OF IT).

There is an important place for rituals and symbols, but incorporating these into your program does not mean you have met your obligation to culturally enhance your services. Utilizing these symbols needs to be done carefully, as misappropriating a tradition or symbol is disrespectful.

7. DIFFERENT WAYS OF KNOWING NEED TO BE INCORPORATED INTO PROGRAMS.

Culture is also about process in terms of traditional ways of knowing. Notions of teacher and student and learning are different than in the more narrowly defined roles held by Western cultures. For example, the use of a sharing circle reflects equality in some First Nations and Inuit cultures and may be more appropriate for Aboriginal youth than a lecture format.

8. HOLISTIC WORLDVIEWS ARE AN INTEGRAL PART OF MOST INDIGENOUS CULTURES.

One way to make almost any activity or program more culturally relevant is to incorporate a more holistic worldview with respect to health and balance. Attending to intellectual, emotional, spiritual, and physical needs will make a program more consistent with traditional Aboriginal values in general. A holistic program strives to incorporate a wellness model that balances all four areas. Spirituality in particular (often misunderstood as religion) is frequently absent from programs.

9. YOUTH NEED ACCESS TO CULTURALLY –RELEVANT MATERIAL, BUT ALSO THE OPPORTUNITIES FOR SELF-REFLECTION.

Incorporating cultural information is not simply about providing youth with particular materials and experiences. It is also about providing them with opportunities to reflect and consider the traditional teachings and to consider the relevance and role of these teachings in a personal way.

10. HISTORICAL AND CONTEMPORARY CULTURAL IMAGES NEED TO BE BALANCED.

Too often attempts to integrate cultural information and images rely solely on antiquated images that reinforce stereotypes. There is a need to maintain a balance between historical and contemporary representations of Aboriginal people.

> *"I didn't realize it at the time, but it was my culture that got me through the rough times... it all comes down to culture."*
>
> *Kristen Hendrick, Elected Councillor, Chippewas of the Thames*

PRINCIPLES INTO ACTION CASE STUDY:
CANADIAN RED CROSS ~ WALKING THE PREVENTION CIRCLE

The Canadian Red Cross *Walking the Prevention Circle (WTPC)* is a program that provides a community with a framework and roadmap for preventing abuse and violence. *WTPC* takes the form of a Capacity Building model that trains prevention educators in their own communities. A critical part of this framework involves providing communities with the language and context to look at really difficult experiences they are facing in order to be able to find healing and a healthy future path. For example, by placing current experiences of violence and abuse into a historical context that looks at contact factors, the Indian Act, and residential schools, a community is better able to understand where their experiences of violence have come from, and in turn better able to be empowered to find solutions.

WPTC takes the form of an intensive three-day community-based program. In addition to introducing a language and context for violence and abuse, this workshop helps to begin developing a roadmap consisting of 10 steps towards creating safe communities. These steps are shown in the diagram below. The depiction of the process as a winding and bumpy road is done intentionally to note that it is not a linear and smooth process.

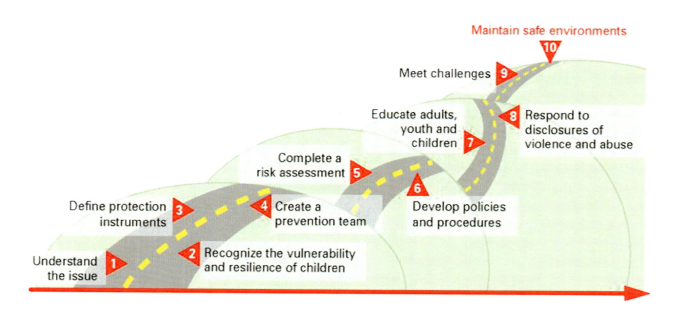

To date *WTPC* workshops have been offered in more than 100 communities from coast to coast to coast. There is a manual to help guide the process. Recent efforts by the Red Cross have focused on increasing the number of Aboriginal Workshop Facilitators available to conduct the workshops. It is noteworthy that the significant uptake of this program has occurred with virtually no attempts to advertise the program, suggesting that the process is one that the communities experience as very positive and helpful. A more formal evaluation is currently underway.

The Walking the Prevention Circle program demonstrates the four guiding principles in the following ways:

Understanding and integrating cultural identity

- ✓ Comes from an historical perspective including Contact Factors, The Indian Act, Residential Schools, Government systems, and popular culture.
- ✓ Uses culturally appropriate teaching tools.
- ✓ Weaves together the Principles of the Red Cross with traditional Aboriginal teachings.
- ✓ Support systems include both traditional and formal systems.
- ✓ The *WTPC* workshop is adjusted to reflect the community's history, traditions and reality; appropriate Elders are incorporated into the teachings.

Increasing youth engagement

- ✓ Youth receive relevant prevention education from community-chosen facilitators who have been selected by the Red Cross and community.
- ✓ Incorporate fun, culturally-based activities and crafts into the workshops to facilitate youths' participation.

Fostering youth empowerment

- ✓ Ties into UN Convention on the Rights of the Child and other international agreements that underscore children's rights to be safe and connected to their culture.
- ✓ Youth and adults are provided with a language to help them name experiences, sort through confusion, and let things go to move forward.
- ✓ The community owns both the problem and solution to violence within their community.
- ✓ Youth receive education on how and where to report, and how to help a friend.

Developing and maintaining effective partnerships

- ✓ Process initiated by a request from the community.
- ✓ Dialogue with the community on needs, capacity, support systems and strengths – are clear about what the Red Cross does offer and does not offer.
- ✓ Participants attend a 3-day *WTPC* workshop and may then be selected by their communities for further training to become prevention educators.
- ✓ Prevention educators are trained and supported by Red Cross.
- ✓ Flexibility based on the community's needs in terms of the structure of the workshop and the language in which it is delivered.

Engaging and Empowering Aboriginal Youth: A Toolkit for Service Providers

PRINCIPLE 2:
INCREASING YOUTH ENGAGEMENT

WHAT IS YOUTH ENGAGEMENT?

Youth engagement is defined as the meaningful participation and sustained involvement of a young person in an activity, with a focus outside of oneself. Appropriate and meaningful youth engagement supports individual development and can serve as a vehicle for community contribution and change.

SUCCESSFUL YOUTH ENGAGEMENT

Through engagement, youth gain a sense of empowerment as individuals and make healthy connections to others, which is associated with a reduction of risk behaviours and increases in positive activities. In addition to the social benefits of these behavioural changes the community gains through the energy and ideas that youth bring to organizations, activities and their relationships with adults (see **http://www.engagementcentre.ca/**). If done properly, youth engagement is a promising strategy for improving outcomes for youth, strengthening organizations, and creating systemic community change.

THE SPECTRUM OF YOUTH ENGAGEMENT

The Centre for Excellence for Youth Engagement describes youth engagement as involving a variety of roles for youth at both the program and organization level. At an organizational level, successful youth engagement involves shared decision-making and collaboration with adults.

> At an **organizational level**, genuine youth engagement moves beyond tokenism towards a process where youth have meaningful involvement in decisions affecting their welfare, in an environment where they can learn from the experience and expertise of adults. Activities or programs within an organization that affect youth are youth-driven and often youth-led, balanced with appropriate adult support. Adults play a critical role in helping youth find their voice and influence in the organization.

> At a **program level**, youth engagement means meaningful participation and sustained involvement in an activity. Youth involved in programs or services that affect them are at the very minimum interested in the program and continue to maintain their involvement in ways that benefit them. For Aboriginal youth, this may involve engaging them in programming by connecting them to their cultural traditions and by creating opportunities for them to be involved in ways that meet their specific needs. Signs of engagement at this level would include consistent attendance and participation, as well as youth reports of finding the program satisfying and meaningful.

CENTRES OF EXCELLENCE FOR CHILDREN'S WELL-BEING

Youth Engagement

THE HEART OF YOUTH ENGAGEMENT: MEETING YOUTH WHERE THEY ARE AT

Programs should be developed with flexibility to meet youth where they feel comfortable. Youth may present in programs with a wide range of needs and motivations that bring them to the service or program. Youth will present with different needs in terms of:

Basic Physical Needs

Empowerment is difficult to attain when basic needs are not being met. At times, program developers or service providers will need to meet the basic needs of youth before they can assist with helping youth build competencies necessary for successful adolescent and adult life. However, these different levels of needs are not linear and youth may become engaged in meaningful activities even while facing challenges around basic needs.

> Meeting youth where they are in terms of needs, motivation, and interests requires flexibility in strategies!

Emotional Wellness and Needs for Healing

Youth may need to heal from their emotional and psychological trauma before engagement can be maximized: "***The greatest issue facing youth participants in the Violence is Preventable project is the need to heal from the painful experience of witnessing violence, before they can feel safe enough to trust the processes they are participating in.***" Shahnaz Rahman, BCYSTH.

Spiritual Trauma

Spiritual trauma refers to the intergenerational impact of residential schools and other assimilation policies and practices. It skews and distorts people's spiritual connections and beliefs about their cultural beliefs and practices.

Their Interests

Youth programming needs to match the interests of youth and it needs to be fun! Integrating culturally relevant material is important, but turning everything into a history lesson will not be engaging for youth. Different youth have different interests, and different levels of awareness with respect to their own cultural heritage.

Their Commitment to an Initiative

An important component of engagement is being able to welcome youth who may differ in terms of their commitment to an initiative at the outset. Providing opportunities of varying intensity and duration will help engage a broader spectrum of youth. In addition, allowing youth to re-enter a program after a period of absence can increase engagement, although the ability to facilitate this will depend on the nature of the program.

PRINCIPLES INTO ACTION CASE STUDY:
NIMKEE NUPIGAWAGAN HEALING CENTRE

Nimkee NupiGawagan is a 10 bed residential treatment program for youth aged 12-17 who are dealing with solvent abuse. Beyond solvent abuse, clients tend to have many other significant challenges. Nimkee provides a 4-month residential treatment program in gender-specific cohorts. It is located in Southwestern Ontario and provides service to youth from Ontario, Quebec, the Maritimes, and Nunavut. The name translates to "Thunderbirds Necklace," which is a metaphor for the youth's healing journey in that the cleansing work of the centre allows the spirit of youth to shine, similar to a rainbow after cleansing rain.

The philosophy of the program is on building strengths to facilitate resiliency. It is holistic in its approach. The program combines the best approaches and principles of addiction treatment with traditional teachings and medicines. There are numerous components to the program including:

Assessment and Treatment Planning – Youth undergo a comprehensive and holistic assessment to identify both strengths and challenges in a range of areas. Treatment plans include individual and group counselling and are holistic in addressing all of the youth's needs (i.e., grief and trauma, behavioural).

Recreation component – Youth engage in a variety of western and traditional recreation, including gym-based activities, and cultural dancing and drumming.

Learning Centre and Work or Volunteer Placements – Youth attend the Learning Centre daily to work on math and literacy. There are opportunities for work and volunteer placements.

Cultural Program – Traditional teachings are woven into every aspect of the program. The philosophy of the program encourages youth to focus on their spirit and reclaiming a healthy spirit. Specific activities (such as sweats) are voluntary in order to meet youth where they are in the process of reclaiming a cultural identity. Youth are required to learn about the options, but not to participate until they are ready. They are provided with the opportunity to do a 2-day wilderness fast at the end of their 4-month stay in preparation for re-joining their communities.

Nutrition Program – A nutritionist helps plan and oversee the dietary component and tailors meals to the youth's needs (i.e., whether they need to increase their weight or decrease it for optimum health).

Health Care – Physical health is addressed both on-site and through community partnerships with an adjacent medical centre. Western and traditional methods of healing are combined.

Aftercare Planning and follow-up – The program works with families and Social Services in youths' communities to build the capacity for a successful return home.

Nimkee has collected outcome data from their clients at 3 month, 6 month and 12 month follow-up intervals. These data indicated positive outcomes across a range of indicators. In addition to reduced substance use (of all types), there is strong evidence that the program is achieving its goal of increased resiliency by improved outcomes in the areas of school attendance, work achievement, family relations, and cultural connectedness.

The Nimkee program for youth addicted to solvents demonstrates the four guiding principles in the following ways:

Understanding and integrating cultural identity

- ✓ Cultural awareness is incorporated into every facet of the program
- ✓ The program is largely staffed with Aboriginal people
- ✓ The Medicine Wheel is used to deliver holistic programming and encourage youth to address all of their needs
- ✓ There are opportunities for weekly sweats and other cultural events (such as feasts and celebration)
- ✓ Youth learn about traditional medicines, and these are used in the program (e.g., the use of teas to help youth through the de-tox phase)

Increasing youth engagement

- ✓ Meet youth where they are at – individual choice is emphasized in activities.
- ✓ Youth are offered opportunties (such as whether to engage in cultural activities) but are not required to do so.
- ✓ When youth are travelling from remote communities, the program attempts to admit them into the program in pairs so that they have a peer from the same community. This pairing helps decrease isolation, particularly if there are language barriers, and provides a support for youth post-discharge.

Fostering youth empowerment

- ✓ Helps participants develop job skills and improve academic outcomes.
- ✓ Offer work placement opportunities and community service hours (for graduation requirements).
- ✓ Strengths-based philosophy that emphasizes youth as the future and their capacity to bring healing to their communities.

Developing and maintaining effective partnerships

- ✓ Family members attend a section of the program at the midpoint where they have the opportunity to participate in parent education classes, recretion and cultural events.
- ✓ Community members are accessed as supports to the youth through community feasts and ceremonies.
- ✓ A partnership with a nearby family-based treatment program ensures that efforts can be coordinated if a youth is at Nimkee and the rest of their family are in the other program.
- ✓ A local trained equine therapist oversees a ½ day/week program at her farm where the youth learn about relationships and trust through working with horses.
- ✓ Nimkee is part of a national group (Canadian Youth Solvent Addiction Committee), which facilitates national coordination for programming, research and advocacy activities.
- ✓ Staff at the centre provide training to other community organization in a range of areas.

ENGAGING YOUTH AT THE PROGRAM LEVEL

> *Young people who participate in programs that strive to engage youth on a number of different levels feel empowered, connected, and valued by adults and their communities. If we look carefully at the heart of all successful youth engagement efforts, we will find strong partnerships with adults who recognize and support the inherent value that young people bring to the success of any program.*
>
> *(Centre for Excellence on Youth Engagement)*

Research in community and program development has consistently shown that people of all ages are more likely to make a commitment to a program when they are involved in meaningful ways in the decisions about programming that affects their lives. Because young people are such a diverse group, and this is especially true for Aboriginal youth, there is no easy way to define youth engagement, nor is there one strategy that will consistently engage all youth in the same way. Youth engagement in programming means that youth become committed and stay involved in meaningful ways in programming over time. Engaging youth in programming is a process that needs to be constantly evaluated and monitored, and flexible enough to meet the needs of a particular group of youth. For Aboriginal youth, having positive role models and engaging them in leadership activities ensures that youth can become more culturally active, feel proud about their accomplishments, and become more involved in their broader community. Youth develop a sense of ownership.

CHALLENGES AND BARRIERS TO YOUTH ENGAGEMENT

Described below are some common barriers that prevent meaningful youth engagement. These barriers can prevent youth from being involved both as participants and as leaders.

Competing Goals and Demands. Youth are busy people. The energy, strengths, and desires of today's youth means they are likely to be involved in multiple activities related to employment, school, peer relationships, and community. For Aboriginal youth in particular, family commitments may be significant and take priority over everything else. Sometimes youth need the opportunity to be involved in smaller ways before they can make a long-term commitment. Flexibility is key to ensuring that youth's participation and engagement in programming is optimized.

Lack of Trust. It is unlikely that successful youth engagement will emerge in the absence of a trusting relationship between an adult and a young person. Engaging youth in programming can be a challenge because of the stereotypes that both adults and young people have about each other. By creating an environment where youth feel safe and respected, trusting relationships with adults and other youth will flourish. As relationships build among youth and adults, youth are more likely to commit to greater challenges and opportunities.

Youth's Individual Histories. Some will find it particularly difficult to develop trusting relationships with adults because of their own histories of abuse and trauma. In some cases, trust may develop over a period of time. In other cases, youth may need the opportunity to get support with respect to their victimization and healing before they are able to develop these relationships. It might be appropriate to make youth aware of other available services or facilitate a referral if necessary.

CHALLENGES AND BARRIERS TO YOUTH ENGAGEMENT (CONT.)

Range of Cultural Connectedness among Youth. In the first principle described in this section we discussed the importance and benefits of youth being connected to a healthy and positive sense of Aboriginal identity. We believe that exposing youth to cultural tradition and practices is a positive way to connect them to their past, but also a way to nurture their spiritual selves. At the same time, we recognize that youth differ greatly in terms of the extent to which they have been exposed to traditional cultural practices and their comfort with these. For youth who have grown up in assimilated households, these issues of Aboriginal identity may be something they have not explored at all. Some may feel very resistant about embracing traditional culture. Depending on their readiness to explore these issues, they may perceive the traditional parts of a program as a barrier to getting involved. One way to address this spectrum of consciousness and readiness is to require youth to learn about traditions, but ensure that it is up to them whether they choose to participate. For example, it is reasonable to expect youth participants (both Aboriginal and non-Aboriginal) to learn about the purpose and philosophy behind smudging, but also important to honour their decisions whether or not to partake.

Poverty. For many youth, limited access to financial resources greatly reduces their ability to participate in programs and activities. Consider waiving costs or finding resources to offer bursaries for youth who could not otherwise participate.

Transportation. Transportation challenges may prevent youth from participating fully in programming, especially when programs are held in remote areas or after school. Providing youth with transportation options, such as bus passes, taxi cabs, or driving youth yourself, will help remove the significant barriers to transportation that prevent youth from fully engaging in programming. Ensure that decisions to transport youth yourself are consistent with the guidelines of your organization due to legal ramifications.

Childcare. Youth may not become engaged to the full extent in a program because of a lack of child care. Organizations should consider providing childcare (and snacks) as part of their programming to reduce these barriers to participation. As with transportation, building these costs into program and project budgets is an important step in resource allocation.

Adult Attitudes. Sometimes adults think that they want to engage youth in a partnership, but may not have done much self-reflection on their own attitudes about the roles of youth and adults in these partnerships. The Centre for Excellence on Youth Engagement has an excellent resource available online that includes questions for adults to ask themselves that will help create self-awareness about attitudes and beliefs they may potentially interfere with being an effective adult ally (available at: --
http://www.engagementcentre.ca/files/alliesFINAL_e_web.pdf)

PRINCIPLES INTO ACTION CASE STUDY:
CRU YOUTH WELLNESS CENTRE

Connections and Resources for U (CRU) was established in 1999 and the name *CRU* was selected by youth for the new Youth Wellness Centre in Saskatoon. A need was expressed by youth and many agencies for a centre where youth could have access to resources and people who would help address various important issues in their lives. Thus, youth from Saskatoon and representatives from various agencies, including the Saskatoon Health Region and the Youth Resource Centre, came together to create *CRU*. They identified physical fitness, emotional and spiritual well-being, personal safety, having something fun to do, and having someone trustworthy to talk to as important components of youth wellness.

CRU programs have been developed to promote youth:

- ✓ Leadership development.
- ✓ Sexual and reproductive health and sexuality.
- ✓ Recreation and leisure.
- ✓ Healthy lifestyles.
- ✓ Cultural awareness.
- ✓ Mental health.
- ✓ Healthy relationships.

Although *CRU* is open to all youth, 90% of participants are of Aboriginal ancestry between the ages of 13-19 who live within the core neighbourhoods. The program staff members at *CRU* are all young Aboriginal individuals. The program assistants are young, not much older than the participants, and are therefore able to connect and identify with the youth and the issues they face. Together these factors have greatly enhanced the success of *CRU's* programming.

CRU currently receives funding from the Urban Multipurpose Aboriginal Youth Centre (UMAYC) program.

CRU is committed to the Youth Engagement and Youth Leadership Model. Working within this model has allowed the centre to develop a "CRU Community" where youth feel welcomed, respected, trusted, appreciated, and valued. This positive environment encourages youth to share their experiences, ideas, and opinions freely. Youth feel that their voices are being heard, and that they have a chance to be involved and to make decisions while gaining leadership skills. *CRU* is a place where youth feel a sense of ownership and positive control. As a result, *CRU* has established itself as a leader in youth engagement in Saskatoon.

By working together, the *CRU* team of youth and adults create programs and opportunities that are meaningful to the participants. The *CRU* Youth Wellness Centre Inc.'s Board of Directors believes in health through the holistic model, which encourages balance in all aspects of one's life. *CRU* has developed some key goals including assisting with the development of young people and to promote healthy choices through prevention and intervention, building positive and supportive relationships in the community and allow youth to develop leadership and responsibility, being proactive in our work and recognize the youth engagement model of community development, and increasing the awareness and involvement of Aboriginal youth issues and culture.

The CRU program for youth demonstrates the four guiding principles in the following ways:

Understanding and integrating cultural identity

- ✓ Recognizes diversity and understanding.
- ✓ Supports positive relationships with self and with others.
- ✓ Promotes various opportunities for young people to become active in their culture through art, dance, stories, crafting, and conferences.
- ✓ Provides safe places to discuss issues that are culturally relevant to youth.
- ✓ Includes activities such as arts and crafts with Elders, field trips, drumming and workshops.

Increasing youth engagement

- ✓ Creates an environment where youth feel respected, valued, and trusted.
- ✓ Provides free activities for youth to participate in physical activity and life skills training (CPR training, food safety certification, conflict resolution, open gym – basketball, volleyball, dance).

Fostering youth empowerment

- ✓ Enables youth to create their own guidelines.
- ✓ Engages young people by creating opportunities for young people to take on leadership roles.
- ✓ Provides Youth Leadership Development training and Youth Facilitator training.
- ✓ Offers resumé workshops.
- ✓ Connects youth with paid or volunteer work experience.
- ✓ Creates opportunities to develop, implement, and deliver workshops to other young people.
- ✓ Provides accurate information that supports youth to make healthy choices.

Developing and maintain effective partnerships

- ✓ Enables access to a Sexual Health Nurse.
- ✓ Presents young people with accurate and appropriate information regarding healthy sexuality.
- ✓ Delivers numerous workshops, discussions, presentations on sexual health/healthy sexuality and healthy relationships.
- ✓ Provides young people with information services and support to manage personal and social obstacles.

STRATEGIES FOR ENGAGING YOUTH AT THE PROGRAM LEVEL

The following strategies and suggestions are a collection of practices that our partners and more importantly, our youth have identified as successful engagement tools.

Start Off on the Right Foot

- Youth are more likely to commit to a program when they are approached by groups or individuals who already have relationships with them.
- Youth need to understand expectations and commitments upfront, and be given time to think them over.

Be Youth Centered

- Engaging youth at the program level requires a balance of work and fun. For example, a peer mentoring program can be structured to include specific structured exercises as well as unstructured time to play board games. Youth who work on youth council should be offered the opprtunity for fun outings or events in addition to their work.
- Program activities should be youth-friendly, with incentives for participation.
- Youth need appropriate adult support to become engaged and stay involved in programming.
- Engage youth in ways that are meaningful to them and in things that will interest them -- the best way to discover youths' interests is to ask them and let them have input into activities!

Incorporate Culture

- Incorporating cultural traditions, such as sharing circles or smudging ceremonies, and including adult mentors or Elders are an important component of youth engagement.
- Aboriginal community partners play a big role in this area and can make the integration of cultural traditions and teachings more authentic than may otherwise be the case.
- Integrating cultural activities should be done with care. For example, smudging should be introduced by an Elder or cultural advisor if the facilitator is not aware of the protocols for this custom.
- Through these traditions, youth experience a greater sense of commitment and belongingness.

Build Trust

- Youth engagement emerges from a mutually beneficial relationship between adults and youth.
- Create an atmosphere where youth feel comfortable speaking for and about themselves.
- Ongoing communication will help build trust and respect.

Be Flexible

- Schedule convenient program meeting times and allow flexible structures. Decisions about scheduling may depend on numerous factors , such as transportation, availability of facilities, other commitments of the youth.
- Program scheduling may need to change from one group of youth to the next depending on these other factors.
- Provide a range of opportunities that facilitate different types or duration of commitment that maximizes the likelihood of a diverse group of youth becoming involved.

STRATEGIES FOR ENGAGING YOUTH (CONT.)[6]

Actions Speak Louder than Words

- Program facilitators need to be reliable and punctual with their attendance.
- This consistency will set the stage for youth to develop trusting relationships, which in turn increases engagement.

Set the Right Tone as a Facilitator

- Youth will pick up on a lack of enthusiasm or genuine commitment from facilitators.
- Facilitator behaviour and attitude provides important modelling and sets the stage for youth to be active participants. Youth will notice if facilitators are saying one thing but acting in a different manner.
- Part of setting the proper tone is to convey an attitude that is non-judgmental, even when participants disclose behaving in potentially dangerous ways.

Provide Training and Specific Strategies for Facilitators

- Facilitators need training and support in engaging youth. These skills go beyond delivering a particular program or curriculum and can be difficult to attain.
- Consider providing facilitators with a manual that outlines concrete steps for engaging youth. For example, the *Youth Launch* program at the CRU in Saskatoon (see case study on page 32 and 33) uses a Youth Facilitator manual that addresses issues such as setting the tone of the group, checking in with the group, setting an agenda in a manner that increases engagement.

Consider Sex Segregated Groups Where Indicated

- There are many types of activities where youth may feel more comfortable and safe participating without the other sex present. For example, the *Youth Launch* program separates males and females for activities such as swimming.
- Other sensitive topics, such as relationships and sexuality may best be approached through a combination of sex-separated and combined groups. Youth may benefit from being able to discuss it in a safe all-girl or all-boy space, but also appreciate the opportunity to hear from the other sex in a larger group format.

Try to Avoid the One-hit-Wonder

- In an ideal world, youth could be re-assured that their involvement is not just for the short-term and that they can count on adults being involved as allies over time. Long-term relationship building helps youth grow and develop, and helps them stay engaged and committed to programming.
- The reality is that many programs rely on funding availability from year to year, and youth age out of programs. It is important to address these issues with youth and look for opportunities for them to be involved in similar positive activities after a particular program ends.
- Facilitating ongoing development for youth beyond what can be offered by a particular program might take the form of making a role for youth in a peer facilitator role or on an advisory committee. At the very least it could involve raising youths' awareness about other opportunities available to them at the end of your program.

---

[6] Although many of our partners contributed ideas for this section, we wish to acknowledge the written materials submitted by Kesha Larocque of *Youth Launch* program at the CRU in Saskatoon.

PRINCIPLES INTO ACTION CASE STUDY:
NEW DIRECTION'S *TERF* PROGRAM

The *Transition and Education Resources for Females (TERF)* program is a unique and comprehensive program for youth who want to exit the sex trade. It is housed at New Directions for Children, Youth, Adults and Families in Winnipeg, Manitoba, and has been in existence since 1987.

Sexually exploited youth who wish to exit the sex trade face many challenges. They tend to have been sexually exploited at an early age and typically by multiple perpetrators. They have faced significant challenges in their families of origin. The exploitation and violence to which they have been exposed have left significant negative impacts. They experience much emotional distress; have significant physical health challenges, and difficulties with the use and abuse of both soft and hard drugs. Their academic achievement tends to be lagging way behind their age-expected level when they enter the program. They face poverty and difficulties accessing safe housing options. Given these massive barriers, it is no surprise that it typically takes multiple attempts for an individual to make this transition. The *TERF* program works with youth participants to attend to all of these needs. The program philosophy combines a holistic approach with a harm reduction model and an understanding of the stages of change. Program components include:

Case Management – youth meet with a case manager at the outset of the program for an assessment that will serve the basis of goal-setting. Case managers undertake a myriad of roles for youth including assessment, counselling and support, referral and advocacy, as long as youth stay connected to the program.

Classroom component – youth have a classroom component every day to help them complete their grade 8 credits, at which time they transfer to an Alternative Education program. Two of their courses – Roots of Empathy and Family Studies – are directly pertinent to their transition process. The classroom component is designed in keeping with a Medicine Wheel format. Other non-credit activities – Transition Group, Substance Awareness and Cultural Teachings – provide an important forum for addressing all of the youths needs.

Support component – although support is integrated throughout the program, there are three designated support workers, at least one of whom is always available by cell phone for crisis intervention. The inclusion of an Elder as a core part of the team provides an important source of support.

Health component – physical health is attended to through the availability of a part-time on-site nurse. In addition, self-care through healthy nutrition and exercise is taught in the program.

Finally, it should be noted that the *TERF* program is not solely available to Aboriginal youth, but approximately 90% of the participants share Aboriginal heritage. This percentage is in line with data on the ethnicity of sexually exploited youth in Manitoba in general. Given these demographics, the program was designed to incorporate cultural relevance from the beginning.

The TERF program for youth exiting the sex trade demonstrates the four guiding principles in the following ways:

Understanding and integrating cultural identity

- ✓ Cultural awareness is incorporated into every facet of the program and is not seen as an add-on.
- ✓ The program expends significant energy recruiting and retaining Aboriginal staff.
- ✓ The classroom component is modeled on the Medicine Wheel and taught in four week segments that represent each of the four directions.
- ✓ The program includes an Elder as a core part of the staff who provides cultural teaching and connection on a weekly basis.
- ✓ Celebratory events that embrace traditional practices such as feasts and powwows.

Increasing youth engagement

- ✓ Meets youth at their state of readiness for change – helps them set realistic goals to keep themselves safer rather than expecting all changes to be made at once.
- ✓ Is designed to allow multiple starts for an individual (i.e., they are not terminated from the program because of a lengthy absence).
- ✓ Provides cash incentives and academic credit for youth who attend.

Fostering youth empowerment

- ✓ Helps participants develop job skills.
- ✓ Helps prepare youth go on to further education in the Red River program for experiential workers.
- ✓ Translates input from participants into changes in subsequent service delivery.

Developing and maintaining effective partnerships

- ✓ The program plays a leadership role in the multi-sectoral provincial strategy to reduce sexual exploitation of youth.
- ✓ *TERF* staff liaise with a number of organizations to increase access to basic needs such as health care and housing.
- ✓ Partnerships facilitate youth being in the program even when incarcerated.
- ✓ Staff played a significant role in the development of the Red River College program for experiential workers.
- ✓ *TERF* staff has worked with a university-based research centre to undertake a comprehensive evaluation[7].

---

[7] For an excellent overview of the program and multi-faceted evaluation, see E. J. Ursel, J. Proulx, L. Dean. & S. Costello (2007). *Evaluation of the TERF Youth and Adult Programs.* Winnipeg, MB: RESOLVE. Available at http://www.umanitoba.ca/resolve/publications/FINAL%20Evaluation%20of%20TERF%20Youth%20&%20Adult%20Program%20Report%202007.pdf

ETHICAL GUIDELINES FOR YOUTH ENGAGEMENT IN ORGANIZATIONS

In considering ways to increase youth engagement at the organization level, there are a number of issues. The following ethical principles were jointly prepared by the Child Welfare League of Canada and the First Nations Child and Family Caring Society, and provide important considerations for increasing youth engagement.

Youth Engagement is Not a Program

- Youth engagement should be viewed as a natural way of working in the organization rather than as a special program.

Contributions Match the Organization

- Young people and adults who are working with an organization should be recruited for their knowledge, skills, interests and commitment to the organizational mission.

One Person Cannot Represent the Many

- A young person should not be considered "the youth voice" at the table – it should be acknowledged that everyone at the table brings different perspectives to the issue.

Debate as a Learning Tool

- Debate is a key element of personal and organizational growth.

Dignity and Safety

- Under no circumstances should young people or adults in the workplace feel that placing themselves in an emotionally, spiritually, physically or cognitively unsafe space is expected or required by the organization.

Avoiding False Expectations

- It is important to be honest about the changing role of youth within an organization including recognizing that there are limitations that correspond to age, experience, education and training.

Balance and Accessibility

- Most people require workplace accommodations in order to support them in making the optimal contribution to the organization – including young people.

(Complete document can be accessed at – http://www.fncfcs.org/docs/declaration_accountability.pdf)

YOUTH ENGAGEMENT – ORGANIZATIONAL AUDIT

It is important to have a snapshot of youth engagement in your organization before undertaking ways to increase it. The following questions were developed by Jocelyn Formsma and Ginger Gosnell (Youth Consultants). These questions will give you an idea of your starting point and possible barriers.

YOUTH AND ADULT ROLES
What has the role of youth been in the project?

- Youth as decision makers for the project's development
- Youth as decision makers for the project's delivery
- Youth as advocates/ speakers/ liaisons on behalf of project

- Youth consulted for advice on the project
- Youth assigned specific roles for the project
- Youth as participants

HOW HAVE YOUNG PEOPLE BEEN INVOLVED IN THE FOLLOWING?
- Design of the project's initial development
- Have held employed positions for the project
- Been involved as volunteers in any aspect of the project
- Received honorariums for their contribution to the project
- Youth are participants in the project

WHAT HAS THE ROLE OF ADULTS BEEN IN THE PROJECT?
- Mentors to youth participants
- Mentors to youth volunteers/employees.
- Decision makers for the project's development
- Decision makers for the project's delivery
- Adults as advocates/speaker/liaisons on behalf of the project
- Supports to youth, but as ultimate decision-makers
- Supports to youth, but with limited decision-making
- Supports to youth, but with no decision-making
- Staff solely dedicated to youth initiatives
- Staff dedicated part-time to youth initiatives

BARRIERS, CHALLENGES AND GAPS – QUESTIONS FOR CONSIDERATION

What are some of the barriers to youth involvement you have encountered, or continue to encounter with this project?

What is/are the cause(s) of the barrier(s)?

What are some solutions your organization has utilized to alleviate the barrier or what are some resources your organization requires in order to address the barrier?

If all necessary resources were available, what other methods would you utilize to remove those barriers?

How Do We Involve Youth in Organizations?

While virtually all organizations agree that youth engagement is important, there are differences in the level of involvement and types of roles that they may envision for youth. Furthermore, the term youth engagement means different things to different people. An important starting point includes an understanding of the different possible roles when deciding which youth role(s) best suit the needs of your organization. The following description was prepared by Jocelyn Forsma as part of her document, *First Steps in Youth Engagement (2002)*.

Youth Council

- Is its own functioning body, sometimes separate from the larger group.
- Has explicit roles and responsibilities, constitution, policies and procedures, etc.
- Has a clear method of selection of Youth Council members.
- Requires structure, resources and dedicated staff.

> *Example*: An Aboriginal Student Council at a secondary school.

Youth Committee

- A part of a larger group.
- Can be a part of the overall or a certain department within an organization.
- Not as structured as a council.
- Fewer resources required.
- Staff works with the committee, but as part of larger responsibilities.

> *Example*: A youth committee at a recreation centre that provides input into activities.

For youth to be meaningful partners, they need to have a voice in all matters – not just for issues pertaining to youth or Aboriginal in nature.

Carey Calder, Native Women's Association of Canada

YOUTH ADVISORY

- Could be ad-hoc or standing.
- Could be an individual, more than one individual, established group or different group every time.
- Gather sporadically to discuss certain issues or provide input / feedback as requested by the organization.

Example: Convening a group of youth to advise on the planning of a conference or other special event.

YOUTH PARTICIPANT

- A youth who has participated in a project, program, or initiative.
- Could be a client or volunteer.
- Could also sit on board or advise certain programs/projects.
- No accountability to a larger group.

Example: A youth invited to sit on a committee to review funding proposals or a regular attendee at a youth program, or drop-in centre.

YOUTH REPRESENTATIVE

- Term "representative" implies that the youth represents the youth membership.
- This designation means that the youth has an extra responsibility to gather information to bring back from a membership (e.g., youth council, board of directors).

Example: A youth representative from the local youth council on the Board of Directors for a Friendship Centre.

YOUTH ORGANIZATION PARTNERSHIP

- Creating a partnership with an existing youth organization, youth council, etc., and requesting the services of their structure for youth consultation and input.

Example: Inviting the youth council from a local Friendship Centre to provide input into the design of a new youth program at a community centre.

> *I am a leader of today, not just tomorrow.*
>
> *Jocelyn Formsma, Youth Consultant*

YOUTH ENGAGEMENT AT THE ORGANIZATIONAL LEVEL: WHAT IS THE ROLE OF ADULTS?

These suggestions are offered from the perspective of a youth leader who has worked in a variety of roles with a variety of organizations.[8]

Assistance in setting up meetings

- Adults can assist in arranging meeting space, utilizing computers and Internet for information purposes, printing agendas and obtaining refreshments.

Guidance in making big decisions

- Although youth need to be the guiding force in decision making, sometimes it is necessary for mentors to step in with advice and/or guidance, especially when dealing with finances. This must only be done with respect for the youth process and at the request and approval of the youth decision makers.

Advocating for youth voice where there currently is none

- Adults sit at a lot of tables or on a lot of committees where youth do not. They have relationships with the current decision makers that create opportunities for them to advocate for youth more effectively sometimes than the youth can. Adults also have the knowledge of the upcoming meetings and can link the value of youth involvement to the possible outcomes of the meeting.

Mentorship – the value of spending time with young people

- Mentorship is time consuming and takes a lot of effort. Spending time with youth and finding out what they think, what they want, and teaching them how to do their work better is not easy. However, one of the most important ways to engage, train and develop young leaders is to simply spend time with them.

Translating youth ideas into action

- Youth have the ideas, the strategies for success, and the enthusiasm. However, they don't always have the resources or the experience to translate those ideas into action. Adults who have the knowledge and access to resources can assist by providing insight and the opportunity to utilize those resources.

---

[8] Adapted from *First Steps in Youth Engagement*, by Jocelyn Formsma (2002).

THE BENEFITS OF ADULTS AS ALLIES

When adults engage youth (i.e., work as "allies"), numerous benefits occur. The following benefits are outlined in the *Adult Allies in Action* publication developed by the Centre of Excellence on Youth Engagement (http://www.engagementcentre.ca/files/alliesFINAL_e_web.pdf).

INDIVIDUAL LEVEL

...Youth

Involving young people in decision-making provides:

- Challenge
- Relevancy
- Voice
- Cause-based action
- Skill building
- Adult structure
- Affirmation

 Leads to...

- Mastery
- Increased social awareness
- Critical thinking skills
- Knowledge application
- Problem solving
- Health
- Compassion

...Adults

There are also vital benefits for adults in adult-youth partnerships.

- Enhanced commitment and energy
- Increased confidence in their abilities to work with youth
- Better understanding of young people's concerns
- Increased sharing of their new knowledge with others outside of the organization

- Strengthened sense of being connected to their community
- Changed perceptions and stereotypes of young people by experiencing youth as competent, legitimate, and crucial contributors

SOCIAL LEVEL

Youth benefit at the social level from:

- Supportive personal relationships
- Expanded social networks
- Opportunities to meet and develop relationships with youth from outside their original peer network

- Opportunities to network with adults and learn about positive relationships through adult role models
- Greater social capital
- Greater peer, family, and school attachment

PRINCIPLE 3:
FOSTERING YOUTH EMPOWERMENT

> *We had had a number of deaths of young men in the community and there was a group of boys that everyone was worried about – boys that were going to go either way. I got them together and told them that I was going to clean up a dump on our community – not an official dump, just a spot where everybody had got into the habit of dumping their trash - and that I wanted their help. In undertaking this, we were going to be taking care of Mother Earth and that was a model for them to use respect and care in their other relationships. I told them that we weren't going to go to the Band Council and we weren't going to get a grant, because you don't need permission from anybody to do the right thing. The sense of accomplishment and pride these boys showed about their involvement in this project was amazing – and all it cost me was a couple of pizza dinners.*
>
> *Jode Kechego, Filmmaker, Land Claims Researcher and Community Developer, Chippewas on the Thames*
>
> **For information on Jode's documentary that was created through this community action progress, see the listing on page 77.*

When you give youth your respect, attention, support and time, and they are engaged in the process and outcome, you are setting them up to allow them to apply their abilities and skills, to address some of their own issues, and to develop new positive opportunities –this is youth empowerment at its best.

When youth experience success and feel trusted and gain some confidence and have a clear understanding of their role, they are more likely to be committed and engaged in a program or activity. Beyond engagement and commitment, they themselves become part of a movement or change process, and become role models to their peers and adults around them.

How do we foster youth empowerment? It can be achieved by providing leadership and life skills, and opportunities to apply these skills to making a difference with others. Youth need a voice in the issues that matter to them and the decisions that affect them. Youth need meaningful access to positive role models. They need to see viable alternatives for leading a meaningful life regardless of the challenges they have experienced.

> *One of the things that struck me as a child was that my own people were not in positions of authority, and I thought that was unacceptable and I guess in a way I felt that in some small way I would be able to change that by going on to higher education.*
>
> *Roberta Jamieson (1953-), First Aboriginal woman lawyer in Canada*

These opportunities can occur in formal program-based ways (such as through a structured mentoring program like the ones described in this section). It can also in more informal and youth-driven ways through community action. It is important to remember that youth-driven empowerment initiatives are not the same as leaving youth to figure these out on their own. Successful youth-driven empowerment initiatives typically have significant adult support. Youth need this adult support to move into empowered leadership roles. If they are forced into these roles before they are ready, their experience will be less fulfilling and meaningful.

In this section of the toolkit we address a number of approaches to empowerment, including ideas for community action, mentoring programs, formal recognition of youth accomplishments, and youth leadership through formal committees and groups.

CREATIVE IDEAS FOR YOUTH COMMUNITY ACTION

The Native Women's Association of Canada (NWAC) has an excellent *Violence Prevention Toolkit* available online (see case study on following pages). This toolkit has the dual goals of providing materials for specific violence prevention workshops, and also providing a framework for youth to become involved in community action. Strategies are accompanied by detailed how-to plans for youth to undertake various initiatives. For example, the toolkit offers the following suggestions for youth community action projects:

1. PRESENT NWAC YOUTH VIOLENCE PREVENTION WORKSHOPS

2. ORGANIZE COMMUNITY MEETINGS

3. PRESENT MATERIAL FROM NWAC YOUTH VIOLENCE PREVENTION WORKSHOPS OR ANY OTHER VIOLENCE PREVENTION MATERIAL AT CONFERENCES AND EVENTS.

4. CREATE RAISING AWARENESS AND EDUCATION PROJECTS

5. ORGANIZE YOUTH WALKS FOR RAISING AWARENESS

6. PUT ON A PLAY OR MAKE A VIDEO TO RAISE AWARENESS ON VIOLENCE ISSUES

7. FORM A YOUTH COMMITTEE OR JOIN AN EXISTING ONE

Use your imagination and creativity to think of many other ways to get involved in violence prevention work in your community and beyond.

For each of these suggestions, the *Violence Prevention Toolkit* offers detailed steps for planning and implementation.

PRINCIPLES INTO ACTION CASE STUDY:
NWAC VIOLENCE PREVENTION TOOLKIT PROJECT

Native Women's Association of Canada's (NWAC) *Violence Prevention Toolkit* is a manual-based approach to empowering youth to raise their own awareness about violence and also to be leaders in violence prevention in their communities. The NWAC Youth Council and the Youth Department developed the toolkit in the spring of 2007 and it was officially launched in December of that same year. This initiative is geared toward youth and service providers in a "Train the Trainer" workshop format. The objective is to enable trainers to deliver these workshops in their own communities. In 2008, a national "Train the Trainer" tour across Canada included training with over 350 participants. The toolkit and training initiative has been made possible by funding from the Status of Women Canada and an extensive and growing network of community partnerships.

Workshop participants are trained in five comprehensive youth-focused workshops that were developed by NWAC youth dealing with the subjects of Domestic Violence, Sexual Assault, Date Violence, Emotional Violence, and Bullying. There is a Facilitator Guide that instructs users on how to deliver the workshops. There are Fact Sheets and Handouts that provide information on all five topics including Community Action (which teaches youth and communities how to get involved in violence prevention). The toolkit also contains Evaluation Forms for delivering the workshops and a CD for electronic versions of all toolkit materials.

The workshops were created to be delivered interactively in a variety of creative ways for participants. There is significant room for flexibility. For example, facilitators can easily incorporate their own cultural teachings within the workshop or include games using the tools provided.

Project Objectives

- ✓ To encourage and promote the use of NWAC Youth Council Violence Prevention Toolkit in communities as part of violence prevention strategy targeting Aboriginal youth.
- ✓ To provide young Aboriginal women and youth in general with a prevention tool that will alert them about possible types of violence they can encounter, ways to recognize their early signs, and ways to empower themselves and break from the victim roles within the reoccurring violence cycles.
- ✓ To empower youth, communities, and community organizations to contribute to combating all types of violence that affect the lives of Aboriginal youth in Canada and decreasing the risk of them experiencing and witnessing violence in their lifetime.
- ✓ To raise awareness about the ways violence affects young Aboriginal women of today in Canada.
- ✓ To empower youth and girls in particular to work on decreasing violence in their communities.

The full toolkit is available at: http://www.nwac-hq.org/en/vpk.html

The Violence Prevention Toolkit initiative demonstrates four guiding principles in the following ways:

Understanding and integrating cultural identity

✓ It is strongly encouraged that Elders are involved in the training workshops and workshops in general. A Community Action insert gives tips on how to approach an Elder.

✓ We also encourage that each community or organization hosting a workshop to build in their own cultural teachings on their agenda's. Smudging or a Healing Circle are some examples.

✓ Includes resources to incorporate historical context (e.g., a Community Action Fact Sheet on Residential Schools.)

Increasing youth engagement

✓ NWAC's Youth Council was instrumental in creating the toolkit.

✓ A limited survey was conducted with youth across Canada to represent youth's voices.

✓ NWAC has sponsored a number of youth at all training workshops.

✓ As of the end of 2008, 138 youth have been trained at the workshops.

✓ Training emphasizes a safe and comfortable environment and includes meals.

Fostering youth empowerment

✓ NWAC's Youth Council has been trained to facilitate the workshops across Canada thus championing the initiative.

✓ Experienced facilitators mentor first time facilitators in the majority of the workshops provided.

✓ Youth Community Action activities are built into the workshops.

✓ There are detailed protocols to support youth empowering activities such as applying for a grant or conference.

✓ 40% of the participants of the training workshops have been youth.

Developing and maintaining effective partnerships

✓ The toolkit offers specific strategies for increasing partnerships in violence prevention, such as how to involve Elders.

✓ Status of Women, Canadian Heritage, Indian and Northern Affairs Canada have all contributed to the initiative.

✓ The Provincial/Territorial /Member Organizations (PTMO's) have worked closely with NWAC in promoting and coordinating some of the workshops.

✓ The City of Ottawa Police assisted in the development of the toolkit in providing expertise and videos for the toolkit.

FINDING YOUR VISION, FINDING YOUR VOICE: A FIRST PERSON PERSPECTIVE ON CULTURALLY-INFORMED EMPOWERMENT[9]

In terms of empowerment, one of the significant movements in the past decade has been the Healing and Wellness movement. This movement has signaled an acknowledgement that many situations of grief have to be dealt with so that individuals can find a path to living a more empowered life. This healing and wellness movement is unique because many Aboriginal communities can find relative success in dealing with the situations of grief that come from a high risk lifestyle, but find it difficult in dealing with sustainable growth for individuals. When an individual is going through the healing process it may be relatively easy to help them find a path to release the issues of grief, anger, shame, guilt for the experiences that they have witnessed with their own eyes. However, Healing and Wellness strategies for Aboriginal people have to also deal with grief that is intangible.

This grief is considered intangible because it is the result of intergenerational trauma. The British Crown and the Canadian Government deliberately and thoughtfully created several extermination and civilization policies in the late 19th and mid 20th century. These policies created grief that is associated with a sense of loss of identity, loss of language, loss of land, and loss of culture. One of the most significant parts of these policies was the Residential school movement. These schools were designed specifically to interrupt this process of passing on the traditional Aboriginal Culture to the children of Aboriginal Communities. Many of these residential schools have been well documented to be institutions where the children were sexually, physically, spiritually, and emotionally abused. Many survivors have conveyed that these institutions were guilty of deliberate torture. Survivors not only carry the grief associated with such victimization but also the intergenerational trauma previously mentioned. The pain and hurt that these survivors carried with them into adulthood has been transferred to their children; they raised them the only way they knew how, with the absence of kindness, nurturing, safety, security and compassion. The patterns present in these dysfunctional families have since transcended several generations to now where there are very dysfunctional communities.

This is why there is such a need to develop innovative processes to circumvent these patterns of dysfunction. The challenge is how to develop means of a sustainable, transformative change. If we examine grief for a moment; grief itself is such an amazing emotion. Nothing else on this earth quite makes us feel this way. Grief is such a powerful emotion because it makes us feel so full and so empty at the exact same time. When an individual is experiencing an intense amount of grief, they feel a sense of loss, hopelessness, powerlessness, and anger. This time of great sorrow is said to be having a loss of Vision. Our eyes are so full of tears we cannot see. We cannot see opportunity; we cannot see a path of living a good life; we do not see what lies ahead; our only focus is on the immediate. An

---

[9] Darren Thomas, co-author, has written this section from a first-person perspective to share his personal philosophy on empowerment. Darren firmly believes that true empowerment for Aboriginal youth, families and communities must be based on a transformation of existing grief. For more about Darren and his work see his biography on page 106.

individual in this state does not always make wise choices; a person in this state is not worried about the impacts their decisions are making on themselves or anyone else. When considering strategies for empowerment, most deal with helping individuals get their sight back. Deal with the tears, dry them. Create new strategies to allow individuals to find a path to healthy living.

However, for sustainable development, you must go deeper into the realm of how these individuals may endure grief. Grief is a part of life and if you send an empowered individual back into a self-defeating environment, their empowerment will eventually fade away. Strategies for these individuals must contain a process where they can help effect change in their families and communities as well. Individuals must find a process to maintain their empowerment. This is where you have to help a person "Find their Voice". Many individuals in a time of self-reflection can tell you exactly what needs to change in Aboriginal communities; they can intensely share with you about what went wrong in their life. Yet they continue to do nothing to contribute to making the change happen. Some of these individuals are sitting in jail, some of them are dependent on drugs or alcohol, and some are just sitting at home. What good is having "Vision" and not having any power? To really effect change, to truly empower Aboriginal communities, you must combine "Vision" and "Voice". Development of strategies that help individuals to clean their eyes is not enough; we have to help them find their voice as well. Their voice is what will drive their vision.

When examining strategies for the entire community, you have to find a collective voice and vision. This Voice is created through collaboration with others. If you create a collective vision and voice then you will ultimately create a truly transformative change, because when you have everyone "buying in" you will see empowered individuals begin to empower their families, which will in turn empower entire communities.

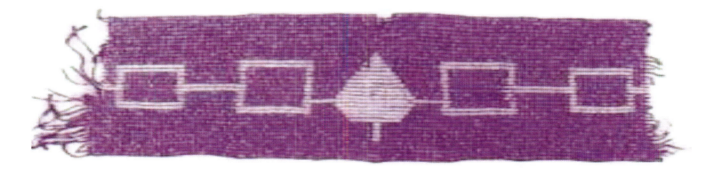

Ayenwatha or the Unity Wampum Belt

Principles into Action Case Study:
BCYSTH Aboriginal Capacity Café

The BC Yukon Society of Transition Houses (BCYSTH) *Violence is Preventable* (*VIP*) Project Coordinator, together with the Aboriginal Education Curriculum Consultant of the Vancouver School Board (VSB), invited School Age Children and Youth, Substance Use Prevention Initiative (SACY) representatives to collaborate, plan and conduct a conference or event in Vancouver which would engage Vancouver urban Aboriginal youth and their parents and caregivers on the issue of violence and substance use in everyday teen life. They were subsequently joined by representatives from the Urban Native Youth Association. The resulting event was an *Aboriginal Capacity Café*, which is an open space for community members to engage in a conversation with youth who have experienced substance abuse, violence, and the realities of teen life. This initial event has been replicated and is now an ongoing initiative. Youth who participate in a Café feel empowered, valued and listened to. As a result, the community feels better able to understand the experiences, and backgrounds that may have been factors in the youth's life choices. For both parties, a Capacity Café creates understanding, appreciation, value and respect.

The *Aboriginal Capacity Café* model has the following objectives:

- ✓ Provide Aboriginal youth opportunities for youth engagement and leadership.
- ✓ Honour and give voice to Aboriginal adolescent views and perspectives particularly regarding substance use and related issues such as violence.
- ✓ Promote among the Aboriginal youth their self-awareness, leadership skills and giving back to the larger community.
- ✓ Increase understanding of youth culture among the students' parents, care-givers, community members and service providers.
- ✓ Reduce the stigma and shame often associated with substance use and violence.
- ✓ Celebrate and build on existing strengths within the Aboriginal community.
- ✓ Enhance participants awareness of drug use and violence issues including resources for additional help.

The structure of the actual events includes:

- ✓ Pre-briefing to develop appropriate questions for students and establish clear confidentiality guidelines and boundaries for all participants.
- ✓ Two simultaneous Capacity Cafés with two facilitators and Aboriginal Youth Advocates to create an open and frank dialogue and maintain confidentiality between Aboriginal students and possible friends and family members.
- ✓ In each Café, participants sit in a circle and 10 Aboriginal youth are spread among the audience in pairs (creating safety). The two experienced facilitators in each Café included one male and one female staff, one being Aboriginal and one non-Aboriginal.
- ✓ Following the Capacity Café, a healing process is conducted in each group
- ✓ Evaluation with adult and student participants.
- ✓ Two youth engagement workshops and one post event youth workshop are facilitated by youth staff. Workshop topics include cultural identity, cultural protocols and teachings, self-esteem, coping mechanisms, and preparation for the Aboriginal Capacity Café
- ✓ The two groups then come back together for testimonials, a quick debrief of what happened in each group and a celebration.

The *Aboriginal Capacity Café* initiative demonstrates the four guiding principles in the following ways:

Understanding and integrating cultural identity

✓ The cultural tone of the events are set by a feast, traditional Smudging ceremony, and an acknowledgement of whose territory the activities were taking place on.

✓ Use of the holistic healing approach and oral tradition by facilitating an informal talking circle.

✓ Four generations attend each event: Elders, grandparents, parents and children.

Increasing youth engagement

✓ The recruitment of youth was facilitated by Substance Abuse Prevention workers, Urban Native Youth Association, and Vancouver School Board staff who already had built rapport and trust with students, which was critical in gathering enough youth to participate.

✓ Provided transportation, free child care and a meal to facilitate the involvement of both youth and adults.

✓ Included a celebration consisting of awards, honoraria, recognition, and door prizes to acknowledge the hard work, commitment and knowledge of everyone who participated.

Fostering youth empowerment

✓ Provided a forum for youth to be the experts of their own experience.

✓ Provided participating youth with a half-day preparation session to prepare them for their role with the larger group.

✓ Structured the event so that youth were not singled out, but rather were seated with a peer and in a circle that did not necessarily include their direct family.

✓ Through the involvement of the Urban Native Youth Association as an organizing partner, youth representatives played a role in the design and implementation of the event.

Developing and maintaining effective partnerships

✓ The event is conducted through a partnership between BCYSTH, the Vancouver School Board (VSB), the Substance Abuse Prevention Initiative of Vancouver Coastal Health (SACY program), and the Urban Native Youth Association (UNYA).

✓ This partnership made it possible to have 22 trained staff on hand for the event.

✓ Each partner brought their specialized expertise to the initiative:
  o SACY – café model, facilitation, youth recruitment and preparation
  o UNYA – cultural aspects, youth recruitment and preparation
  o VSB – promotion of event to Aboriginal parents, caregivers, and students
  o BCYSTH – administrative and event planning assistance

YOUTH EMPOWERMENT THROUGH MENTORING

> *It is vital in today's modern society to not only tell our youth you care and are concerned about them.... you have to show them."*
>
> *Darren Thomas, Community Educator and Motivational Consultant, Six Nations*

THE VALUE OF MENTORING

Mentoring is an excellent way to empower youth, whether they are taking the role of mentor or mentee. Through the power of a positive and healthy relationship, youth being mentored have access to a strong role model, and someone with whom they can discuss future plans, worries, and celebrate successes. Working in the role as mentor, youth have the powerful experience of helping another peer make good choices and feel connected, which in turn builds the mentor's sense of him or herself as a leader and role model. Mentoring is not a unidirectional enterprise; both parties gain valuable experience and skills in the process.

> *Mentoring is giving a person the freedom to understand what it is they could possibly choose for self. The mentor gives them ways to look at an object to gain some understanding or knowledge of the object, identify the responsibilities for taking care of the object and know that their choice is solely their responsibility. You as the mentor empower them to take responsibility for their choices rather than this person coming back and saying, "It's your fault for getting me into this mess I'm in right now.*
>
> *Randy Johnson, Storyteller from Mohawk Six Nations, cited in Traditional Lifestyles Mentoring Report for the New Orators Youth Project. Grand River Employment and Training, 2002.*

CULTURAL FIT

Personal or social mentoring fits well with the values of many Aboriginal cultures in several ways:

- Mentoring recognizes that all individuals can learn from each other and that teaching is not limited to those with a formal designation.

- Including activity-based mentoring in addition to talking reflects different ways of knowing.

- Mentoring by definition is a more holistic approach to a person than focusing on one area of skill. It is also a means of transferring knowledge from a traditional perspective.

- Traditionally, mentoring-types of relationships were formalized in many Aboriginal cultures through specially designated "aunties" and "uncles".

- The type of relationship that emerges through mentoring provides an excellent forum for teaching and strengthening cultural aspects.

Engaging and Empowering Aboriginal Youth: A Toolkit for Service Providers

GUIDING PRINCIPLES FOR DEVELOPING MENTORING PROGRAMS

The following recommendations were provided in a paper *Mentoring Programs for Aboriginal Youth*, published in Pimatisiwin: A Journal of Aboriginal and Indigenous Community Health.[10] The authors of this paper underwent a series of 10 interviews with Aboriginal program developers and a focus group with 5 participants. Through this process they identified three guiding principles:

1. Mentoring should not be seen as a stand-alone, narrowly targeted program, but rather as an activity that is entirely supportive of community values and goals and that is fully integrated with other community education, healing, and capacity building activities.

2. Mentoring should be embedded in existing programs.

3. A community advisory group should be established at the outset of any mentoring program to inform and guide the development, evolution, and maintenance of the program.

> *We have these things where we understand each other and we talk about school and other important things.*
>
> *Mentee, Uniting Our Nations Peer Mentoring Program*

PRACTICAL CONSIDERATIONS

In addition to following the guiding principles, there are practical strategies that can increase the success of a mentoring program:

- Mentoring in groups instead of on an individual basis may be a good fit culturally, and can also address the potential difficulty of recruiting enough mentors for one-on-one mentoring.

- All mentors, be they adults or other youth, require some training and orientation to the mentoring process.

- The extent to which program organizers can look after the logistics (such as meeting time and place, inclusion of meals) will facilitate regular and productive mentoring sessions.

- Allowing sufficient time for the recruitment and selection of both mentors and mentees and choosing appropriate candidates will increase the likelihood of the program's success.

---

[10] Klinck, J., Cardinal, C., Edwards, K., Gibson, N., Bisanz, J., & da Costa, J. (2005). Mentoring programs for Aboriginal youth. *Pimatisiwin: A Journal of Aboriginal and Indigenous Community Health, 3,* 109-130. Available at www.pimatisiwin.com. Although this article was written in reference to mentoring programs, it offers excellent recommendations that are more broadly applicable to any type of program development.

EXAMPLES OF CULTURALLY RELEVANT MENTORING PROGRAMS

SCHOOL-BASED MENTORING BY COMMUNITY ADULTS: NEW ORATORS AUNTIES AND UNCLES MENTORING PROGRAM

The *Aunties and Uncles* mentoring program is a mentoring program using adult community mentors. It focuses on children ages 10 and up with the goal that the Aunties and Uncles (mentors) can secure positive relationships with the participants before they begin the transition into being young men and women. The community mentors engage in a range of programming from cultural teachings to traditional arts, crafts, and games, and the development of a positive relationship is primary. The understanding of adolescence as a rite of passage is central to the organization of the program. It has been offered primarily through elementary schools on the Six Nations of the Grand River, although there are extension activities offered at the local secondary schools as well. There are typically 15-20 students involved at a time, but logistics of the program have differed to meet the needs of a particular site and the local support. For example, at one site the administration really believed that this work was vital to student social development so they provided time during school. In other sites most of the programming was done after school or as summer camp sessions.

Philosophy: In many Aboriginal cultures the understanding of raising children was that it was the responsibility of the entire community. In modern times, concepts such as these are being lost due to the number of families and communities losing touch with their original teachings. It was believed that many carried the responsibility of assisting the parents. The extended family as well as any member of the community, if they were older, would be acknowledged as auntie, uncle or grandparent. This was understood and all Elders were respected.

During the time when a young man's voice starts to deepen and when a young woman would start her moon time (i.e., commence menstruation) it was said that a rite of passage would occur. For a young man the Uncles and Grandfathers would sit the nephew down and begin to outline his future responsibilities of being a man, walking with him through the challenging years of adolescence, spending time with the young man and challenging him about his roles and responsibilities of being a man. The purpose was to ensure that values, traditions, and identity were set forth as a source of courage, strength, honour and pride for the future. For a young woman, the Aunties and Grandmothers would take on this responsibility, guiding the young woman into womanhood by teaching her about her connection to the natural world and the responsibilities she carries as a woman. As a result of modern society and the desire to become educated by today's standards, this rite of passage is very rarely done. Families send their young men and women to school to figure out for themselves what they are good at, what they want to be when they grow up, and to learn on their own what their responsibilities and values should be. Since many educational institutions do very little to empower Aboriginal people about their identity, young people struggle a great deal with the challenging years of adolescence. Mentoring helps support youth during this time of transition.

School-Based Mentoring by Older Peers:
Uniting Our Nations Peer Mentoring Program

The *Uniting Our Nations* peer mentoring program supports the development of healthy and positive relationships between younger secondary students and peer mentors from older grades. Students meet on a weekly basis at school during lunch time and engage in a range of activities together, sometimes with a cultural focus, and other times with general activities enjoyed by youth in this age group. The initial time commitment is once a week during the common lunch period, for one school semester, although most students choose to be involved for the whole year. The link with older students helps smooth the transition from elementary to secondary school for the younger individuals, and connects people with similar interests and backgrounds. Although the program began as a paired mentoring strategy, it has evolved to group-based mentoring, which the students seem to enjoy, and is a structure that helps minimize the impact of absenteeism. Mentors receive a full day of training prior to the program starting and a manual to assist them in their role.

A unique aspect of the peer mentoring program is the involvement of an Aboriginal adult mentor from the community who comes into the school several times per semester, typically to facilitate a teaching circle with the mentoring participants. Unlike most programs that are two-tier (mentee-mentor), mentors and mentees can learn from stories, examples and actions from the community mentor. Having a community mentor in place has helped affirm traditional cultural values with youth and places some ownership and responsibility of the program on the community. This community mentor helps provide support to the school mentors, incorporates cultural teachings into the program, provides a role model to all of the youth involved, and provides the opportunity for the youth to become connected to another healthy adult in their community. For other Uniting Our Nations programs see the case study on page 74 or go to www.youthrelationships.org.

Mentoring training. Printed with permission

PRINCIPLES INTO ACTION CASE STUDY:
DND – JUNIOR CANADIAN RANGERS PROGRAMME

The Department of National Defence *Junior Canadian Rangers (JCR) Programme* emerged out of the observed need to provide meaningful activities for young people in isolated communities. The *JCR Programme* offers young people (ages 12 to 18) in remote and isolated communities across Canada a unique opportunity to participate in a variety of fun and rewarding activities in a formal setting. The *JCR Programme* strives to strengthen remote and isolated Canadian communities through an altruistic, responsible and practical youth programme that embraces culture and tradition, promotes healthy living and positive self-image, and reflects the proud military legacy of the Canadian Rangers. There are three components to the training the *JCR* receive:

Traditional Skills: Traditional skills are those that expressly take into account the background and culture of the *JCR* in any given community. Elders are often involved in teaching these important skills where applicable, and community members are sometimes invited to participate. *JCR* learn the significance and relevance that Traditional skills still have today, at the personal and community levels. Skills that risk being lost are reinforced through teachings that strengthen connections among youth, adults and Elders. Examples of traditional skills include hunting, fishing, local language, traditional music and dance, traditional cooking and spiritual ceremonies.

Life Skills: Life skills provide *JCR* with important lessons that help them to become healthy, well-respected and responsible members of their communities. This part of the curriculum is also adaptable according to the particular needs of the local community. In certain communities with high-risk youths, for example, qualified facilitators might teach suicide prevention and intervention, while others focus on staying drug-free or speaking in public. Examples of life skills include good nutrition, staying in school, drug and alcohol abuse awareness, and citizenship. The PHASE (*Preventing Harassment and Abuse through Successful Education*) program could also be taught to all *JCR* as part of the Department of National Defence's commitment to providing a safe learning environment. *PHASE* is facilitated via the Community PHASE Facilitator utilizing a Facilitator Guide in conjunction with a 51-minute video that is broken done into 11 sections or vignettes, along with games and youth activities that promote dialogue. A sharing circle is regularly employed to provide *Junior Canadian Rangers* with a safe and familiar forum to express themselves and to feel accepted for their experiences, thoughts, feelings and comments.

Ranger Skills: Ranger skills offer *JCR* the training required to become capable, skilled and active members of their communities. This training provides valuable "real life" experience on the land, where mastering the core skills of travelling, surviving, and communicating helps create confident and resourceful youth. Ranger skills are taught by experienced individuals, and involve practical exercises and hands-on training. It is here that *JCR* learn about the important role their instructors serve in the Canadian Forces and become acquainted with the customs of the military, including marching, saluting and care for their uniforms and equipment. Although the instructors are part of the Canadian Forces, the *JCR* are not.

There are approximately 3,400 *Junior Canadian Rangers* in 119 remote and isolated communities across Canada. Many of these youth are Aboriginal and some speak a language other than English or French.

The Junior Canadian Rangers Programme demonstrates the four guiding principles in the following ways:

Understanding and integrating cultural identity

- ✓ A third of the program is specifically devoted to teaching traditional cultural values and skills that are relevant to the particular community.
- ✓ There is a strong emphasis on skills required to live off the land.
- ✓ There is significant flexibility to accomodate the needs and traditions of the particular community.
- ✓ Elders and other cultural leaders are included in the program's design and delivery through the Adult Committee.

Increasing youth engagement

- ✓ The *JCR* Programme offers an option for structured and fun youth programming in areas where there are few alternative programs.
- ✓ The *JCR* Programme incorporates fun, culturally-based activities and skills development to increase youths' participation.
- ✓ There is no cost for participation to reduce barriers for interested youth.
- ✓ *JCR* are encouraged to take an active role in the Patrol decisions, and the youth elect their own peer leaders within their Patrol.

Fostering youth empowerment

- ✓ Youth empowerment is developed through structured teaching of meaningful skills. Skill development is seen as the primary tool to enhance the positive self-image of the JCR: to create a sense of competence, usefulness, belonging, and control of their own futures.
- ✓ The life skills and ranger skills portions teach specific skills that will be applicable to later employment roles.
- ✓ There is an emphasis on healthy and safe decision making in a range of areas.
- ✓ *JCR* have extensive opportunities to expand their personal experience, face and overcome challenges, and to try out new roles and responsibilities in a safe environment.

Developing and maintaining effective partnerships

- ✓ The *JCR* Programme was developed as a partnership between the DND and INAC.
- ✓ *JCR* are taught by qualified Canadian Rangers with the assistance of adult volunteers and other members of the Canadian Forces.
- ✓ Each *JCR* Programme patrol is overseen by a local Adult Committee of approximately 8 members. Members typically include respected community members such as the tribal council elder, the mayor, the local RCMP officer, and social workers or teachers, and Canadian Rangers.
- ✓ Specific modules have been developed in conjunction with partners who have special expertise – for example all PHASE modules on the prevention of harassment and abuse were developed with the Red Cross RespectEd team.

THE IMPORTANCE OF RECOGNIZING YOUTH STRENGTHS AND ACCOMPLISHMENTS

Recognizing youth in ways that are meaningful to them can make a lasting impact that goes beyond their involvement in a program. Consider ways to recognize youth publicly within their peer group settings or at school, and privately, by taking the time to get to know them on a personal level. Recognizing youth for their successes tells them they are important, significant people. Try to look at the award through the eyes of the young person to determine what would be meaningful and important to them. Programs and services can recognize and celebrate youth talents and accomplishments in a variety of ways:

* Youth who graduate from programs or reach certain milestones should receive a certificate of accomplishment for their successes. These certificates may be particularly meaningful for youth who are not on track to receive a high school diploma.

* Have a final recognition ceremony or party for youth participants and invite their family and close friends. Cultural components can be built into these ceremonies (e.g., inviting a drumming group to sing an honour song).

* Recognizing youth for their successes by publishing their names in a newsletter, website, or in the local newspaper after completion of the program is a positive way to recognize participants. Remember to get consent before publishing identifying information.

* Write youth a letter of reference or nominate them for a larger community or agency award.

* Don't forget to ask youth themselves what a meaningful recognition for participation may be. Try to avoid using generic awards that may be convenient or because you have a large supply on hand. Interests and preferences of young people change from one developmental stage to another so it is important to keep that in mind when selecting appropriate recognition awards.

* Youth can be nominated for numerous awards to recognize their accomplishments more formally. A number of awards are listed on the National Aboriginal Achievement Foundation website at http://www.naaf.ca/html/home_e.html. Another award is Lead the Way? Program administered by the National Aboriginal Health Organization. This Program selects a number of youth each year who are positive role models to others and honours them for their achievements, leadership, and innovation. In turn, these youth conduct numerous community visits and presentations. More information is available at: http://www.naho.ca/rolemodel/English/nomination_generalinfo.php. Youth can be encouraged to talk to student services as their schools to learn more about other local awards programs.

LEADERSHIP OPPORTUNITIES THROUGH ORGANIZATIONS WITH YOUTH GROUPS:

Youth seeking to further their leadership skills and experiences may wish to seek involvement with the youth council of an organization. For example, Friendship Centres typically have either a youth council or a youth representative on their boards. Encouraging youth to seek out and apply for these positions (with your support) is one way to foster the development of these leadership skills.

Most National Aboriginal Organizations have their own national youth councils and they all have individual processes for selecting their members. To find out more about these youth councils go to:

- Assembly of First Nations (AFN) - http://www.afnyouth.ca
- Métis National Council (MNC) - http://www.metisnation.ca/youth
- Inuit Tapiriit Kanatami (ITK) - http://www.niyc.ca
- Native Women's Association of Canada (NWAC)– http://www.nwac-hq.org/en/youthcouncil.html
- Congress of Aboriginal Peoples (CAP) - http://www.abo-peoples.org/youth.html
- National Association of Friendship Centres (NAFC) - http://www.nafc-aboriginal.com/ayc.htm

> *"Youth have to be invited, encouraged and supported before they can feel comfortable in leadership roles."*
>
> Hazel Cardinal, Executive Director, Helping Spirit Lodge Society, Vancouver, B.C.

Principles into Action Case Study:
RCMP – Aboriginal Pre-Cadet Training Program[11]

This *Aboriginal Pre-Cadet Training Program* (APTP) offers Aboriginal youth the opportunity to work as sworn peace officers with the RCMP and the First Nations Chiefs of Police Association (FNCPA). This initiative is for older youth compared to the other programs profiled in this toolkit. Through the APTP, youth (ages 19 –29) undergo 3 weeks of training at the RCMP Depot in Regina followed by a 14 weeks posting at a detachment near their community. The program provides selected candidates with hands-on experience in the RCMP's training program, an inside look at the life of a police officer and ample opportunity to do meaningful work in the community. APTP assists Aboriginal youth in developing discipline, confidence, self-respect, teamwork and adjustment to a non-Aboriginal environment.

The three week portion at the RCMP Depot in Regina includes training on:

- ✓ Collaborative problem-solving skills.
- ✓ Law enforcement.
- ✓ Public speaking.
- ✓ Cultural diversity.
- ✓ Facilitation of Safe Community Workshops in communities.

There are also elements of physical fitness and drill which promote teamwork and provide students with long-term strategies to meet personal fitness goals. Graduates leave the Academy with a greater appreciation of policing and the role of Aboriginal people in the RCMP.

> *"APTP creates a better understanding of the RCMP in Aboriginal communities and in gaining the interest and attracting Aboriginal applicants as regular members of the RCMP. For many participants the Program is the first step in the applicant process and has encouraged many past participants to pursue a career in the RCMP."*
>
> *Sgt. Ed Jobson*
> *National Recruiting Program*

After graduation, students are posted to RCMP detachments near their home community where they work alongside seasoned police officers for 14 weeks. The duties and activities the student engages in are at the discretion of the detachment commander who ensures that students are not exposed to any hazardous situations. Activities and duties vary depending on the need of each region but the students will get a first-hand look at a career in policing.

---

[11] In 2009 the name of this program was changed from the Aboriginal Youth Training Program to its current name.

The Aboriginal Pre-Cadet Training Program demonstrates the four guiding principles in the following ways:

Understanding and integrating cultural identity

- ✓ The Depot component integrates traditional culture and practices (e,.g., youth participate in sweats during the program).
- ✓ There is an emphasis on raising awareness of the role of Aboriginal officers in the RCMP.
- ✓ The program promotes careers in law enforcement for Aboriginal youth, which in turn leads to more Aboriginal people in the RCMP. The increased representation adds to the knowledge of the organization and also enhances the way that the RCMP can respond to the needs of Aboriginal communities.

Increasing youth engagement

- ✓ Pariticpants have the opportunity to get hands-on experience that will be relevant for a career in policing.
- ✓ The APTP offers a stipend for participants.
- ✓ The program offers youth an opportunity to get an inside look at the RCMP, reducing barriers to those who might be interested in pursuing a career with the RCMP.

Fostering youth empowerment

- ✓ Youth empowerment is developed through the acquisition of skills.
- ✓ Beyond the specific law enforcement skills taught, there are also general employment skills (such as conflict resolution and public speaking) that will be applicable to any field.
- ✓ The community-based portion helps participants gain important experience as community leaders through the facilitation of safety workshops and other activities.
- ✓ Many of the youth participants have gone on to have careers with the RCMP or other law enforcement agencies.

Developing and maintaining effective partnerships

- ✓ The APTP is a partnership between the RCMP and the National Aboriginal Policing Services.
- ✓ Youth are specifically taught skills for collaborative approaches to resolving community problems.
- ✓ Detachments who host APTP participants receive support from the Program Managers, Divisions, and other National Policy Centres to increase the success of the participants during the community policing portion of the program.

PRINCIPLE 4:
ESTABLISHING AND MAINTAINING EFFECTIVE PARTNERSHIPS

Effective partnerships are perhaps the single most determinative factor in providing enhanced services for Aboriginal youth. Although the stakeholders involved will differ from project to project, there are different types of partners typically involved. Some of these partners may be more or less involved at different stages of a project, but giving careful consideration to roles and communication is essential for successful program planning and delivery. Partnerships typically include:

Service providers - Service providers typically provide the setting and programming. In this toolkit we are addressing service providers who may or may not have specialized services for Aboriginal youth, or may simply count these youth among their general youth participants.

Researchers - There may be external researchers involved with your project, or this may be a role handled internally. Research questions, methodology, and evaluation should be determined by all of the partners collectively, rather than being imposed.

Educators - If the program is set in schools, there may be many educational partners. These may include teachers, support staff, First Nations Counsellors, administrators, and school board personnel. Understanding these different roles is essential for working effectively with schools.

Funders - Funding partners are often overlooked between grant applications, but play an integral role in the success of programs. Funders should be updated and kept informed of projects and activities.

Community - There may be partners from the Aboriginal community (including Elders) who are not parents of the youth involved. It is important to choose partners carefully to ensure that they are held in respect by their own communities and will be appropriate role models for the youth involved.

Family - Family can be involved in a variety of ways, including service development, delivery, recruitment, transportation, etc. Some level of parent involvement is considered a best practice component for youth programming in general, and for Aboriginal youth in particular.

CONSIDERATIONS FOR DEVELOPING PARTNERSHIPS

Much of the future success of partnerships depends on selecting appropriate community partners and getting these partnerships off to a good start. The following considerations have been shared by Aboriginal partners to offer some starting points for non-Aboriginal individuals and organizations seeking partnerships with members of Aboriginal communities. Partnerships and teams must be reflective of the community they serve.

RECOGNIZE THAT BUILDING RELATIONSHIPS TAKES TIME

All partnerships have to start somewhere. Although good work can come out of new partnerships, established partnerships emerge over the course of years of collaboration. Committing to collaborate over a period of time sets the stage for the development of these relationships.

ACKNOWLEDGE DIFFERENCES IN MANDATES AND CONFLICTING PRIORITIES

Each partner brings different perspectives and mandates to the table and acknowledging them up front and appreciating these differences will strengthen your partnerships. For example, in planning a school-based youth engagement initiative, there may be a number of different stakeholders with different views and concerns. The school-based First Nations support staff may want to open the opportunity to as many youth as possible while the facilitators may have an optimum number in mind to foster group dynamics. The school administrators may be most concerned about how much school youth will miss. If the program is being funded by research dollars, then researchers may face other pressures due to financial constraints. Acknowledging these sources of potential tension and brainstorming solutions as a group can help build trust and prevent misunderstandings.

MAKE RELATIONSHIP BUILDING A PRIORITY — NOT AN AFTERTHOUGHT

Relationship building takes resources to accomplish. Try to set aside the necessary resources both in terms of time, and also budgets. Try to include these activities in your funding proposals when possible. There are ways to build relationships that do not require a lot of expense:

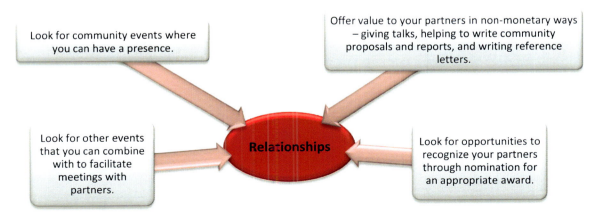

RECOGNIZE THAT THERE WILL BE BUMPS ALONG THE ROAD.

As in any relationship, individuals and organizations working together will encounter stressful times and misunderstandings. Recognizing that these bumps are inevitable will go a long way towards not abandoning a project in the face of tension among partners. A commitment to work through these differences and retain a focus on the youth you are trying to support can help you through these difficult periods with partners.

BE MINDFUL OF DIFFERENCES IN TIMELINES AND WORKING STYLES.

> *"Praise, flattery, exaggerated manners, and fine, high-sounding words were no part of Lakota politeness. Excessive manners were put down as insincere, and the constant talker was considered rude and thoughtless. Conversation was never begun at once, or in a hurried manner.*
>
> *No one was quick with a question, no matter how important, and no one was pressed for an answer. A pause giving time for thought was the truly courteous way of beginning and conducting a conversation."*
>
> *Chief Luther Standing Bear (1868-1939)*
> *Oglala Lakota Chief, writer and actor*

Community partners, educators, and researchers often have different timelines, which affects the pacing of the collaborative work. Researchers may suddenly need input and support letters to apply for a grant, while community partners would like more time to consider the request. Community partners and researchers may want input from educational partners, but find it difficult to access them at particularly busy times during the school year or during holidays. Researchers and non-Aboriginal community partners may be looking for immediate input on an issue at a meeting, while their Aboriginal partners would prefer an opportunity to reflect on the issue and potentially seek input from others. Acknowledge these challenges up front and recognize when you are asking people to make a decision or provide input without sufficient time. It is also important to recognize that there will be times when you are unable to apply for a grant or meet a deadline because of the realities of these community partnerships. Scheduling regular meetings may help anticipate some of the crises of having no time to submit something.

SELECT COMMUNITY PARTNERS BASED ON THEIR CREDIBILITY WITHIN THEIR COMMUNITIES.

Community credibility is the single most important characteristic of your community partners. Often, role models and leaders in the community may not be the individuals with a particular job or title. Once you have positive relationships with members of the community, ask their advice for identifying other partners.

INVOLVING YOUTH AS PARTNERS REQUIRES A CONSCIOUS COMMITMENT

Youth are important partners in all aspects of programming. A large part of this section of the toolkit is devoted to engaging and empowering youth. It is also important to involve youth in research, as discussed on page 90 in the research section of this toolkit.

THINK ABOUT THE TYPES OF INFLUENCE YOU NEED ON YOUR TEAM

Beyond credibility, it is important to think about the type of expertise and authority you may need on your team. For example, the Red Cross *Walking the Prevention Circle* program addresses the following questions when working with a community to develop a prevention team. Depending on the nature of your organization and program delivery, some or all of the following questions may be important to consider:

- ☑ Who are the decision makers?
- ☑ Who has knowledge of legal systems?
- ☑ Who determines budget allocations?
- ☑ Who is responsible for communications?
- ☑ Who oversees programs and services for children?
- ☑ Who will hold the group accountable?

BE AWARE OF THE DIFFERENCE BETWEEN BUILDING RAPPORT AND BEING OVERLY INTRUSIVE

In an effort to seem friendly and interested, it is possible to inadvertently be intrusive in the types of questions you ask. For example, asking someone you have just met, "Why don't some Aboriginal people consider themselves Canadian?" is inquiring into a deeply personal and political area. These types of conversations may be more appropriate once you have established a relationship of trust and openness over time, but not in the early rapport building phase of a relationship.

UNDERSTAND THAT YOUR INITIAL WORDS AND FORMAL CREDENTIALS WILL MEAN VERY LITTLE TO THE WAY IN WHICH YOU ARE PERCEIVED AS A POTENTIAL PARTNER

Your credibility in working with Aboriginal partners will be based on how you conduct yourself at meetings and how your actions match your words. Your formal credentials and job title mean very little compared to your integrity and the extent to which you meet your commitments. There is a historical context to meaningless promises being made by non-Aboriginal individuals (often in the context of extending "help,") and your partners may be understandably wary.

KNOW THERE IS DIVERSITY OF ABORIGINAL POLITICAL ORGANIZATIONS AND VIEWPOINTS IN CANADA

There are numerous Aboriginal political organizations in Canada, and there may be areas of significant disagreement among these groups (just as there are among non-Aboriginal political organizations!) It is respectful to have at least a preliminary understanding of the different organizations and affiliations when you begin to work with Aboriginal partners, or use your partners to help you understand this landscape.

Successful Partnerships Require Strong Communication Plans

Open and ongoing communication provides an essential foundation to healthy and respectful partnerships, but it is difficult to maintain. It is important to recognize that communication with various stakeholders requires different approaches. For example, email updates may work well with educators, but a community-based face-to-face meeting might be more effective with parents. Scheduling regular meetings that coincide with important junctures of a project or key decision-making times can help keep things on track. It is also important to create a variety of ways for individuals to provide input into the project (e.g., not requiring written submissions, for example).

Talk About the Type of Partnership You Are Seeking and Clarify Roles

Be clear about the extent to which partners are being asked for input, have decision-making power, or are merely expected to rubber stamp decisions that have already been made. Asking people to serve in an advisory capacity where they do not have a true voice can lead to resentment and relationships difficulties. Not all partnerships will include equal responsibility, decision-making and involvement, and that is okay. The important part is to clarify these roles as much as possible at the outset (while recognizing that partnerships and projects are ever-evolving).

Ensure that Women's Voices are Represented

Women are key decision makers in many First Nations, Métis and Inuit communities. They are role models for youth and need to be given a voice on committee and partnerships.

Develop Specific Strategies for Engaging Parents and Guardians

Many community organizations recognize the importance of parental / familial involvement in youth programming, but have difficulty engaging families. This issue is not unique to programming for Aboriginal youth, but is faced by service providers and educators in general. It is important to remember that parents may not get involved for a variety of reasons, and not assume a lack of interest. There are a number of strategies that can be used to increase parent engagement:

- Be flexible about when you schedule events and meetings with parents – if most parents work during the day, choose an evening or weekend. If possible arrange for childcare and refreshments to facilitate attendance at events.

- Go to the parents and community if possible – for example, set up a booth at a Fall Fair on the local Reserve or partner with Local Friendship Centres on and off the reserve.

- Consider bestowing exceptional youth with a violence prevention leadership award. Community members often enjoy attending an event where youth are honoured.

- Use multiple parent engagement strategies to engage a wider range of parents.

- Recognize the unique circumstances of parents from urban versus reserve communities and adapt your engagement strategies for each group.

- For specific ideas see *Engaging Aboriginal Parents in the School System* on page 76.

PARTNERSHIPS IN ACTION – ACCESSING ELDERS

Elders play important roles in traditional cultures, as advisors, mediators, mentors, and knowledge keepers. They are an important partner for effective programming. The following advice was written for youth who are approaching Elders, but it contains helpful advice for both youth and adults wishing to access this valuable community resource. It is reprinted with permission from the NWAC *Violence Prevention Toolkit* (see case study starting on page 40).

TOOL
HOW TO APPROACH AN ELDER

Whereas different communities have their own unique ways of approaching their Elders and incorporating traditional teachings, the following is some general advice provided by Elder Irene Lindsay who was helping the young women of NWAC's Youth Council on their journey in developing the Violence Prevention Toolkit for Aboriginal girls.

1) Bring a pouch of tobacco or a little rock to an Elder as a way to approach them

2) Ask if they can meet with you

3) Consider Elders as alternatives to other options

4) Think about the ways in which an Elder can help

5) Give Elders respect and time

6) Elders can introduce you to traditional aspects - ask the Elder about traditional ways of dealing with the problem

7) Understand the value of Elders in your culture and your community

8) There are some things out there - there is an Aboriginal community you should be proud of

9) Don't forget - TRADITIONAL APPROACH WORKS!

For a more in-depth guide, see Interviewing Elders: Guidelines from the National Aboriginal Health Organization *at* http://www.naho.ca/english/documents/InterviewingElders--FINAL.pdf.

CARING ACROSS THE BOUNDARIES INITIATIVE

Many of the partnership strategies discussed in this section are based on the assumption that organizations have at least a few partners within the Aboriginal community with whom they can collaborate. For some organizations, collaborating with Aboriginal partners might be a completely new area and one where you do not feel you have any expertise at all. There is an excellent initiative called *Caring across the Boundaries* that can provide support to organizations in this regard.

Caring across the Boundaries is an interactive workshop that facilitates collaboration between First Nations child and family services agencies and the voluntary sector. The program was developed based on research which found that First Nations children and youth on reserve have almost no access to the broad range of prevention and quality of life services provided by the voluntary sector[12]. A key finding of the research was that both First Nations child and family service providers and voluntary sector agencies want to ensure First Nations children and youth are able to access culturally appropriate voluntary sector supports. Identified barriers to collaboration expressed by voluntary sector and First Nations agencies include:

Barriers to Collaboration Include:

- Lack of time
- Lack of networking opportunities
- Hesitancy to initiate contact
- Lack of funds
- Lack of knowledge, information and understanding about each other

During the *Caring across the Boundaries* workshop, participants work together to identify strategies to overcome these barriers. This activity quickly reveals that the vast majority of the barriers cited can be readily overcome. *Caring across the Boundaries* provides a process for participants to make new connections and create joint visions of future collaboration.

The curriculum is designed to help First Nations and the voluntary sector learn more about each other in a safe, supportive environment and begin breaking down barriers to collaboration. The training provides space for participants to make new connections, network and create joint visions of future collaboration. The program is intended for individuals working for non-profit, public service, philanthropic and government agencies engaged in activities related to child, youth and family service and individuals working with First Nations social service agencies both on and off-reserve. Training is offered in 1.5 day workshops consisting of a half day primer session and a full day collaboration session.

More information about the initiative can be accessed at:
http://www.fncfcs.com/projects/caringAcrossBoundaries.html

---

[12] FNCFSC, 2003

SECTION 3: OPPORTUNITIES AND CHALLENGES IN SCHOOL-BASED PREVENTION PROGRAMMING

WORKING WITH SCHOOLS

Many organizations and groups see the benefit in working with schools to offer prevention programming and other services to youth. There are many advantages to partnering with schools and other educational settings. Some of the advantages include:

Access to many youth: Although the highest risk youth are not typically found in a mainstream school setting, it is an efficient way to offer services to large numbers of low-to-medium risk youth.

Sharing of resources: Providing services in the school setting can result in shared resources and logistics, such as the use of space and possibly transportation (e.g., if your group meets at lunch).

Increasing school engagement through school-based programming: For many Aboriginal youth, school is a difficult place and may not feel very welcoming. Providing a different type of experience in the school setting can lead to more positive feelings about school in general. School connectedness increases the likelihood that they will attend regularly and experience success.

OUR PROJECTS USED THE EDUCATIONAL SPHERE IN DIFFERENT WAYS AND TO VARYING DEGREES:

Universal prevention in a school setting: The *Fourth R: Uniting Our Nations* (see case study starting on page 74) provides youth in mainstream school settings with a variety of opportunities to be involved with violence prevention, including an extracurricular peer mentoring program, a number of for-credit course opportunities, and a transition conference for grade 8 students preparing to start secondary school.

Capacity building with educators: Partnering with educators can lead to increased awareness of violence and the impacts of violence among those professionals who work in schools with youth on a daily basis. Considerations for conducting professional development with educators are outlined starting on page 57.

Liaising with schools to provide access to services for youth: The *Violence is Preventable* (VIP) Project of the BCYSTH works with schools to link children and youth who have been exposed to domestic violence to appropriate provincial *Children Who Witness Abuse* programs run by transition homes and women serving organizations (case study starting on page 78).

Creating educational opportunities within a specialized service setting: The *TERF* program at New Directions (see case study starting on page 30) helps youth who are exiting the sex trade to attain academic success by offering courses and credit opportunities integrated with counselling, job skills, and life skills.

What Can Schools and School Boards Do?

> *My nation was ignored in your history textbooks - they were little more important in the history of Canada than the buffalo that ranged the plains.*
>
> *Chief Dan George (1899-1981)*
> *Salish Chief, actor, and author*

Honouring Aboriginal ways of knowing can be initiated in schools by making several choices to:

- develop new initiatives and strengthen current policies related to cultural affirmation and school climate;

- encourage healthy and meaningful relationship-building opportunities among all school community members;

- develop and strengthen partnerships to facilitate shared decision making;

- support access to and development of practical, relevant, and authentic resources reflective of traditional and cultural knowledge;

- support teachers and students in efforts to actualize Aboriginal content and perspectives and the perspectives of diverse cultures in learning experiences;

- learn from and about Aboriginal peoples;

- with partners, develop long-term, comprehensive plans to support language and culture programs, such as Aboriginal languages and Native Studies;

- establish goals and monitor desired progress toward ensuring teaching and learning as culturally affirming and appropriate; and, practice equitable employment at all levels reflective of the school community (i.e., administration, staff, governance, volunteer);

- diversify the traditional membership in high schools to include Aboriginal Cultural Advisors and Elders.

This requires increased awareness and respect for local traditions and protocols, and increased flexibility when these role expectations and responsibilities vary from the roles of others in schools.

Adapted from a Saskatchewan Ministry of Education document available at:
http://www.sasked.gov.sk.ca/branches/pol_eval/community_ed/docs/hs2004splus.pdf)

Section 3: Opportunities and challenges in school-based prevention programming
Engaging and Empowering Aboriginal Youth: A Toolkit for Service Providers

65

WHAT CAN EDUCATORS DO TO BETTER ENGAGE ABORIGINAL YOUTH?

Research demonstrates that a number of factors contribute to the academic success of Aboriginal students:

- Educators who have high expectations and truly care for Aboriginal students.
- Classroom environments that honour Aboriginal students' culture, language, world view and knowledge.
- Teaching practices that reflect Aboriginal learning styles (see next page for example).
- Schools that have strong partnerships with the Aboriginal community.

How can classroom teachers integrate culture into the classroom? The following table shows an example of how the seven Grandfathers (also known as the Good Life teachings or Seven Virtues) can be operationalized in a classroom setting[13].

Table 1
Ojibwe Good Life Teachings and Implications for Education

Teaching	Implications for Education
Respect	Having high expectations for the Aboriginal student and honoring their culture, language and world view in our schools
Love	Demonstrating our belief (as educators) that all Aboriginal students can and will succeed through our own commitment to their learning-teaching styles
Bravery	Committing to change in our school curriculum through including the contributions, innovations and inventions of Aboriginal people
Wisdom	Sharing effective practices in Aboriginal education through ongoing professional development and research that focuses on imbuing equity
Humility	Acknowledging that we need to learn more about the diversity of Aboriginal people and accessing key First Nations resources to enhance that state
Honesty	Accepting that we have much to learn from one another and reviewing the factors involved to encourage change in the education system (increased parental-guardian involvement, teacher education)
Truth	Developing measurable outcomes for Aboriginal student success and using them as key indicators of how inclusive our curriculum and pedagogy really are

Note: The seven good life teachings are values/principles that are central to the Anishtnabek

---

[13] The information on this page and the figure on the next page are taken from a document on the Ontario Ministry of Education and Training website, available at:
http://www.edu.gov.on.ca/eng/literacynumeracy/inspire/research/Toulouse.pdf

WHAT CAN EDUCATORS DO? HONOURING ABORIGINAL LEARNING STYLES

While it is inappropriate to make generalizations about the learning styles of *all* Aboriginal students, there are learning styles that fit with traditional styles of education among many Aboriginal peoples.

Appreciating the Learning Styles of Aboriginal Students

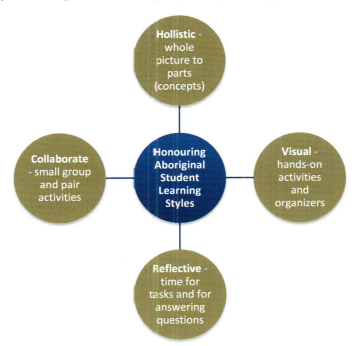

Values and traditions of Aboriginal peoples support more holistic learning approaches that do not rely solely on written modes of communications. There are a number of considerations that teachers can take into account in matching the learning styles of Aboriginal students.

> *"Much of Canadians' day-to-day lives involve contributions from Aboriginal people. Without indigenous knowledge, Canada would not be Canada. There are numerous contributions including a variety of foods, forms of government, materials, transportation routes and inventions. If even more indigenous knowledge had been adopted earlier, women would have had the vote, medicines would have been available and clean water and air would be the norm. Much in Canada would be different if society embraced some traditional Aboriginal values A whole community would be involved in looking out for all children, we would value knowledge more than information and our goal would be to grow old and wise so we could teach our children. People wouldn't be in retirement homes, they would be in the classroom."*
>
> *Cindy Blackstock*
> *Executive Director, First Nations Child and Family Caring Society*

CAPACITY BUILDING WITH EDUCATORS

Schools can be supported to provide a more welcoming and engaging environment for Aboriginal youth in a variety of ways. Programming and resources are important, and external organizations can play a leadership role in developing culturally relevant materials and assisting in developing culturally responsive environments. Equally important are initiatives that increase educator capacity to respond to the needs of Aboriginal youth, through increasing educators' training, awareness, and comfort with Aboriginal perspectives. If your organization wants to help foster this professional development of educators, it may be useful to:

Work closely with partners from the educational system.	<ul><li>The educational system is a very structured system with highly specific policies, protocols, procedures and guidelines. Learning to work with the educational system can be like learning a foreign language and culture.</li><li>Working with educational partners from the outset can increase the likelihood that a program will be adapted and used, rather than presenting a finished idea to the local board.</li><li>Having educators on any planning committee can help you shape your initiatives in a way that maximizes the likelihood of their success.</li></ul>
Provide opportunities for educators to process new information that may be uncomfortable to them.	<ul><li>Learning about the history and context of Aboriginal peoples in Canada is not simply learning dates and facts.</li><li>It involves coming to terms with a national history that includes systematic attempts to colonize, assimilate, and at times, extinguish the peoples who are indigenous to the land.</li><li>Many Canadians do not have accurate information about the reality and extent of residential schools, for example, and learning about this part of our shared history can cause feelings of denial, overwhelming sadness and shame.</li><li>Learning opportunities for educators need to balance the provision of information with the ability to process the information emotionally.</li></ul>
Balance history and context with specific strategies for educators.	<ul><li>Supporting educators to become more responsive to Aboriginal students requires them to have a greater awareness of shared history and cultural traditions, but at the end of the day, they also require specific, action-oriented strategies.</li><li>An understanding of history and context helps educators understand the importance of incorporating Aboriginal perspectives into the classroom, but many educators are at a loss of how to accomplish that goal.</li><li>Specific strategies, lesson plan ideas, and resources will support educators in applying their new awareness to the students in their classroom.</li></ul>

Raise awareness about the daily realities of Aboriginal youth.

- There is much diversity among the lived experiences of Aboriginal youth.
- Educators would benefit from learning more about the strengths and challenges of the particular communtiy with which they are working.
- For example, in some northern communities, youth may be attending high school hundreds of miles from their home communities and be billeted by non-Aboriginal families.
- An awareness of these types of stressors will help educators connect with youth in a caring and compassionate manner.

Provide self-reflection opportunities for educators.

- Many non-Aboriginal Canadians have not thought much about their relationship to Aboriginal peoples.
- Dr. Susan Dion (York University) refers to this position as the "perfect stranger" -- if you have no relationship to a group of people, you also have no obligation to learn more or play a role in redressing historical injustices.
- Dr. Dion argues that educators need some awareness about their position of perfect stranger before they can learn more about Aboriginal peoples in an ethical way.
- Seesee *Dion, S. (2007). Disrupting molded images: Identities, responsibilities, and relationships -- teachers and indigenous subject material. Teaching Education, 18, 329-342.*

Help educators understand the importance and relevance of incorporating an Aboriginal perspective.

- Some educators think they do not have a role to play because they are not Aboriginal themselves or do not teach a particular type of course.
- Encourage a shared sense of responsibility by framing the lack of awareness of Aboriginal perspectives as a social justice issue.
- In addition, tying the professional development to school board and Ministry mandates can help impart a sense of importance and obligation.

Provide instruction in how to integrate content.

- Once educators recognize the need to better integrate Aboriginal perspectives into their classroom, they may still benefit from specific instructions and guidelines.
- The framework for levels of integration depicted on the following page is a useful paradigm for educators and may help prevent situations where well-meaning educators contribute further to the general lack of awareness by only addressing the first level of integration.

Section 3: Opportunities and challenges in school-based prevention programming
Engaging and Empowering Aboriginal Youth: A Toolkit for Service Providers

69

LEVELS OF INTEGRATION OF MULTICULTURAL CONTENT

Educators can integrate multicultural content into their classrooms and lessons in a number of ways. The level of integration exists along a continuum from more superficial to truly integrated.[14]

Level 1
- **The Contributions Approach**
- Focuses on heroes, holidays, and discrete cultural elements.

Level 2
- **The Additive Approach**
- Content, concepts, themes, and perspectives are added to the curriculum without changing its structure.

Level 3
- **The Transformation Approach**
- The structure of the curriculum is changed to enable students to view concepts, issues, events, and themes from the perspectives of diverse ethnic and cultural groups.

Level 4
- **The Social Action Approach**
- Students make decisions on important social issues and take action to solve them. Includes components of transformation approach, but students are required to make decisions and take actions related to the concept, issue, or problem studies in the unit.

---

[14] This information has been adapted from a summary prepared by James A. Banks. The entire document is available at http://resources.css.edu/Diversity Services/docs/LevelsofIntegrationofmutliculturalcontent.pdf.

Suggested DVD Resources on Aboriginal Issues, Identity and History

There are many DVDs available to help you further your understanding of Aboriginal issues, identity, and the shared history between Aboriginal and non-Aboriginal peoples in Canada. The resources listed below are provided as a starting point, but not intended to exclude other excellent resources.

Movies Available on DVD:

Tkaronto (2008)
100 min. drama

Tkaronto is a reflective and provoking exploration of two Aboriginal 30-somethings, Ray and Jolene, who make an unexpected connection at the pinnacle of a common struggle: to stake claim to their urban aboriginal identity. Metis director Shane Belcourt conveys the loss and struggle of the two lead characters in a film that is moving and at times, humorous. (www.tkaronto.net)

Muffins For Granny (2008)
88 min. documentary

Distributed by Mongrel Media, *Muffins For Granny* is a remarkably layered, emotionally complex story of personal and cultural survival. McLaren tells the story of her own grandmother by combining precious home movie fragments with the stories of seven elders dramatically affected by their experiences in residential schools. McLaren uses animation with a painterly visual approach to move the audience between the darkness of memory and the reality that these charismatic survivors live in today (from Youtube Trailer)." Available from amazon.ca.

Three Nations One Story Part I: The Aftermath of Assimilation (2008)
45min. documentary

Produced by Crossing Borders Productions, Three Nations One Story reflects on the raw reality of the struggles young people face in the post-residential school era with Chippewas of the Thames, Munsee-Delaware Nation and Oneida Nation of the Thames being the profiled communities. Part I: The Aftermath of Assimilation takes a close look at the internal struggles people deal with and how three communities came to be plagued with addictions, violence and funerals. With the residential school era coming to a close in the late 1960s (though the last one did not close until 1996), generations of families were left with trauma, dysfunction, poverty and violence. Raw interviews symbolically parallel a youth-driven garbage clean-up to reveal deep issues and shows some simple things people can do to help themselves. (www.crossingbordersproductions.com).

Where are the Children? Healing the Legacy of Residential Schools (2008)
27 min. documentary

Describes, through interviews with former boarders, the conditions and state of the residential aboriginal schools from the late nineteenth century to the 1990s. The conditions were harsh and children were forced to forget their Aboriginal heritage. Produced by the Legacy of Hope Foundation. (www.legacyofhope.ca).

FNCFCS has an excellent list of suggested resources at: http://www.fncfcs.com/pubs/recommendReading.html#fng

Programming Integrated into the School Setting

> "If school boards would mandate staff to deliver in-house programs for First Nations youth, there would be greater participation and sustainability for the projects than the research model which depends on the irregularity of funding agencies. The challenge for some research-based projects is that they are essentially run off-site from where the program is implemented and cannot be woven in tightly into the fabric of the school."
>
> *Ray Hughes, Fourth R National Education Coordinator*

Programs that are integrated into the educational system tend to have better sustainability in that the responsibility for funding and conducting these services is shifted from the community to the school, or at least shared between the two. Community organizations still play a critical role in the development and delivery of these services, but the shared sense of responsibility increases the likelihood of success.

Many community organizations develop programs and services with the goals of these being implemented in schools in an ongoing manner. Designing programs with an understanding of the realities of the school system from the outset will promote the implementation and eventual adoption of a program rather than trying to make the program fit after it has been developed.

For example, all of the provincial Ministries of Education have curriculum documents that standardize what is taught in a particular course at each grade level. The purpose behind these documents and guidelines is to ensure that students throughout a province or territory are receiving comparable levels of education. The implication of these curriculum documents is that teachers may be resistant to teaching material and objectives that do not match the curriculum expectations of their course. The extent to which an activity or initiative can be shown to support mandated curriculum expectations will increase the general receptivity to the initiative. Activities that can be shown to support literacy and numeracy will also be more positively received.

The checklist on the following page was developed to identify areas that may be useful to address in designing programs that you want to be successfully implemented in schools. Obviously it is not necessary to be able to answer each of the questions in a particular way, but thinking about these areas will help you in planning your program and service delivery.

These questions will assist you in planning and implementing school-based prevention activities. An awareness of the different areas covered here will also better prepare you to meet with school board personnel.

CHECKLIST FOR IDENTIFYING AREAS OF ALIGNMENT WITH SCHOOL BOARD POLICIES AND INITIATIVES

POLICIES	○ Have you checked the Provincial Ministry of Education policies on Aboriginal education and aligned your objectives to match their policy statement?
	○ Are you familiar with any school board policies or initiatives underway with which you could align?
	○ If you are working with a particular school, are you aware of the school's policies or initiatives?
	○ Are there teacher federation mandates or requirements that align with your work?
PARTNERSHIPS	○ Is there a local school board committee responsible for Aboriginal Education initiatives? If so, can you present your ideas to this committee early in the process to assess interest, feasibility, and potentially identify appropriate partners?
	○ Is there a particular superintendant/consultant with a portfolio for Aboriginal Education? Can you get in touch with this person early on in your planning?
	○ Are there other community organizations already successfully partnering with the school board that you could use as a resource or mentor? Ask them about their failures in school-based programming as well as their successes.
	○ Can you recruit an educator to be on your advisory committee or project development team? This individual will be able to assist you with the alignment process throughout all phases of development and delivery.
	○ Is there someone at the school or board level who is known to be a "champion" of this type of initiative?
LINKS TO CURRICULUM	○ Have you decided which grade levels and areas you will be targeting with your initiative? Can you identify particular Ministry curriculum expectations that your initiative matches?
	○ If your initiative involves community-based individuals doing presentations or facilitating activities, can you develop follow-up activities that teachers can deliver, which match specific curriculum expectations?
	○ Can you utilize recognized literacy strategies in your materials or the follow-up activities?
ROLE OF SCHOOL PERSONNEL	○ Have you met with school administrators to determine the school's current programming?
	○ Are administrators on board with your programming and will they support their teachers and staff in these initiatives?
	○ Do teachers have a role in the delivery of the program? As supervisors? Co-facilitators?
	○ Will teachers require specialized training and / or resources? If so, who will pay for these costs?
ROLE OF YOUTH	○ Do youth have a role in the delivery of the program?
	○ Will they require training? Support? Resources?

PRINCIPLES INTO ACTION CASE STUDY:
THE FOURTH R: UNITING OUR NATIONS

There are many challenges facing Aboriginal youth in the current education system. The residential school system played a large role in negating the protective factors of culture and community for many youth, resulting in widespread mistrust of the formal education system. This history laid the foundation for youth being disconnected from school, but the lack of engagement is propagated by the current system in several ways – youths' culture is not reflected in the curriculum, there are few Aboriginal adult role models in the school system, and there is a lack of awareness about relevant historical and cultural issues among educators. As a group, these youth continue to experience early departure from high school at disproportionate rates.

Over the past four years our team of researchers and educators has worked closely with Aboriginal youth, educators, community members, and the Thames Valley District School Board (TVDSB) to develop a number of strength-based programs. Collectively, we refer to these initiatives as *Uniting Our Nations: Relationship-based programming for Aboriginal youth*[15]. These initiatives have two goals. First, by making changes in the school setting (through the incorporation of culturally-relevant curricula, developing mentoring and supports, and raising educator awareness), we have worked to change the salience of school as a place of learning for Aboriginal youth. Second, by providing these youth with opportunities to explore their leadership capabilities, engage in culturally enhancing activities, and be connected to role models in their schools and communities, we have worked to foster their learning spirits and empower them. Some of the individual components of *Uniting Our Nations* include:

✓ A peer mentoring program for secondary students that involved older Aboriginal students mentoring younger ones to develop a positive relationship and assist the younger students make a successful transition to secondary school. For more information on the *Uniting Our Nations* mentoring program see page 49). A mentoring program for youth in grades 7 and 8 is being piloted during the 2008-2009 school year. The elementary program uses young adult mentors to work with small groups of youth.

✓ *A First Nations Cultural Leadership Course* that combines grade 9 and grade 11 students into the same classroom to work on one of two credits (grade 9 general study skills or grade 11 peer leadership). This class incorporates peer mentoring, cultural enhancement activities (such as drum making and community outings), and relationship skills. The students are encouraged to work together, learn from each other, and develop strong relationships.

✓ Twice yearly Grade 8 transition conferences that bring together students from urban and Reserve elementary schools to engage in culturally-relevant activities, discuss concerns about high school, and connect them to positive supports available in the high schools they will be attending. Senior students from the peer mentoring program and *First Nations Cultural Leadership Course* play a primary role in planning and hosting the conferences.

---

[15] *Uniting Our Nations* was developed as part of Strategies for Healthy Youth Relationships, featuring the *Fourth R* school-based programs. More information about these programs is available at www.youthrelationships.org. A DVD resource featuring youth reflecting on their school experience and issues of identity is forthcoming.

The *Uniting Our Nations* initiatives demonstrate the four guiding principles in the following ways:

Understanding and integrating cultural identity

- ✓ Cultural teachings are incorporated in the secondary peer mentoring program through the involvement of adult community mentors to share traditions.
- ✓ Peer mentoring training includes traditions such as smudging and a component on cultural identity.
- ✓ Culturally enhancing activities are built into the classroom-based courses such as drum and mask-making, community guest speakers and culturally relevant videos.

Increasing youth engagement

- ✓ Youth are recruited for potential involvement through pre-existing relationships with First Nations Counsellors and other youth.
- ✓ Twice annual grade 8 transition conferences are held to help prepare elementary students for high school and to begin the process of engaging them with culturally-relevant opportunities available.
- ✓ School engagement and success is increased through the provision of opportunities to gain academic credit in culturally-relevant study skill and peer leadership courses.
- ✓ The program addresses barriers for involvement by addressing logistical issues through the provision of transportation and meals.

Fostering youth empowerment

- ✓ Youth in high school are trained to be mentors to younger youth and supported in this role.
- ✓ Older youth in the mentoring program and *First Nations Cultural Leadership Course* are encouraged and supported in taking leadership roles in planning and conducting the grade 8 Aboriginal Transition conferences.
- ✓ Youth have been hired as consultants on projects when possible.
- ✓ Youth have been invited to attend conferences and co-present with program developers.
- ✓ Youth involved in the projects have presented on a youth panel at educator training events and in a DVD developed for similar purposes.

Developing and maintaining effective partnerships

- ✓ The programs have emerged through a partnership between the Thames Valley District School Board and the Fourth R team at the CAMH Centre for Prevention Science.
- ✓ Adult Community Mentors come into the schools to support the Peer Mentoring program.
- ✓ An Advisory Committee of First Nations Counsellors and administrators meets regularly to discuss future directions and problem-solve challenges.
- ✓ Teacher training activities are developed and conducted to increase educator awareness of Aboriginal cultures and history to assist teachers in better supporting Aboriginal students.
- ✓ Community-based parent engagement activities are delivered to coincide with local community events.

ENGAGING ABORIGINAL PARENTS IN THE SCHOOL SYSTEM

One challenge faced by educators is that parents of Aboriginal students may not be very engaged or involved in their children's schooling process. This lack of engagement is an important issue to address because parental involvement supports better learning outcomes for youth. To better understand the lack of engagement, it is important to understand the challenges and ineffective strategies for engagement, as well as the more effective approaches. The information on this page and the next has been drawn from an excellent report stemming from the *Parent and Education Engagement Partnership Project* in British Columbia. The project involved province-wide consultation and documentation of practices (both ineffective and effective). These findings are documented and available in a report that is available on the internet.[16] The main findings are summarized here. Although this project was conducted specifically in relation to parent engagement in schools, the principles are more widely applicable to engaging parents in community-based services.

BARRIERS:

A number of barriers have been identified that interfere with Aboriginal parents being engaged and involved partners in the educational system. Some of these relate to the parents' situations and experiences and others relate to characteristics of the school system. These include:

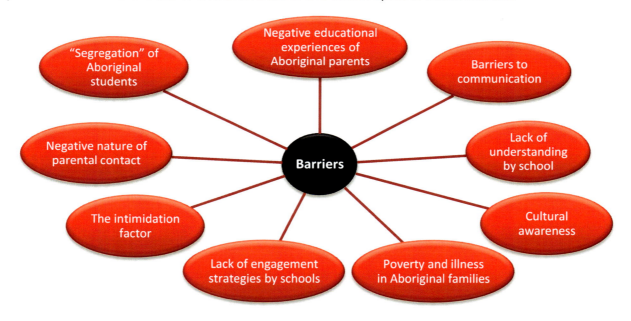

---

[16] R.A. Malatest and Associates, Ltd. Parent and Education Engagement Partnership Project: A discussion paper. July 30, 2002. Available at http://www.bced.gov.bc.ca/abed/reports/parent_engage.pdf.

INEFFECTIVE STRATEGIES:

The same report noted a range of unsuccessful strategies identified by stakeholders. These include:

- Meeting with no reason
- Limited duration programs / initiatives
- "Tokenism" – such as having one parent represent the "Aboriginal point of view" on a committee
- Insufficient promotion of strategies and initiatives

TYPES OF PARENT ENGAGEMENT ACTIVITIES

Parent engagement strategies documented by the *Parent and Education Engagement Partnership Project* include a variety of approaches. Some schools use governance strategies and initiatives. For example, an Aboriginal Education Committee that has some decision-making power would be considered this type of strategy. Another strategy is the development of Aboriginal support services, which designates individuals who have the responsibility of liaising with families and promoting cultural events at schools to which parents and families are invited. Aboriginal support services might also help develop curriculum resources and work directly with students to support their learning. School orientation activities were another parent engagement strategy highlighted. Typical activities of this type include an orientation day for new Aboriginal students and their families, and parent handbooks. Finally, cultural awareness and culturally inclusive activities promote parent engagement.

GUIDING PRINCIPLES FOR EFFECTIVE PARENT-EDUCATOR RELATIONSHIPS

1. Respect for Aboriginal culture is an essential element of an engagement strategy.
2. When schools are welcoming and friendly, Aboriginal parents are more likely to feel comfortable engaging with the school.
3. Parents and school staff working cooperatively to develop strategies and programs based on principles of partnership builds strong relationships.
4. It is imperative that Aboriginal communities are encouraged to become partners in making decisions regarding Aboriginal programs and services.
5. District leadership is important in the support and development of engagement strategies.
6. Measureable targets allow implemented strategies to be assessed for their effectiveness.
7. One strategy will not "fit all".
8. Strategies to engage Aboriginal parents require administrators and teachers to develop partner relationships with Aboriginal parents based on mutual respect and trust.

PRINCIPLES INTO ACTION CASE STUDY:
VIOLENCE IS PREVENTABLE PROJECT AND ABORIGINAL STUDENTS

The "Violence Is Preventable" (VIP) project was initiated in 2004 in British Columbia by BCYSTH with the goal of establishing a province-wide system that would provide children and adolescents with school-based support and education related to issues of domestic violence. The objectives of the VIP project are:

- ✓ To break the silence of domestic violence by making it safe for children and youth to speak up in schools about domestic violence and the issues that impact their lives.
- ✓ To increase teacher, school staff, parent and student awareness about violence in relationships and its effects on child witnesses.
- ✓ To facilitate partnerships between schools and communities in order to respond to the emotional, social, academic and psychological needs of children exposed to domestic violence.

BCYSTH offers central coordination of the VIP initiative including:

- ✓ Resource development.
- ✓ Development and delivery of VIP training for CWWA counsellors.
- ✓ On-going support and guidance to CWWA counsellors and their member agencies.
- ✓ Province-wide awareness-raising, sustainability planning and advocacy.
- ✓ Support for Aboriginal, multicultural and other identified communities.
- ✓ Community development strategies and support.
- ✓ Training of program facilitators.

There are three key activity services to schools:

1. *Awareness Presentations:* To educate educators, parents and other adults (e.g., foster parents, public health nurses, child care providers, and others who have a stake in the healthy development of our children) about children and youth's exposure to domestic violence.

2. *Violence Prevention Presentations:* Classroom presentations (kindergarten to grade twelve) so that children and youth can learn about domestic violence. In addition to learning about domestic violence, these presentations also include topics such as unhealthy vs. healthy relationships, communication skills, and self-esteem.

3. *Group Interventions:* For children and youth who have been exposed to domestic violence, multi-week psycho-educational groups are held for students in the school setting so that they may have the support needed to cope with the impact of domestic violence on their lives.

Although the program was always intended to provide culturally-relevant support for specific cultural groups, BCYSTH formally documented some of their strategies for increasing relevancy with Aboriginal communities in the 2007 revision of their manual.

The *Violence is Preventable* initiative demonstrates the four guiding principles in the following ways:

Understanding and integrating cultural identity

- ✓ Includes background information and history of domestic violence both common to families who are not Aboriginal and specific to Aboriginal histories and experiences.
- ✓ Glossary of common Aboriginal terminology for CWWA counsellors.
- ✓ Provides resources and handouts such as "Elements of Aboriginal Domestic Violence" that can be printed and distributed to Aboriginal students and partners.

Increasing youth engagement

- ✓ Youth receive culturally relevant psycho-educational support from CWWA counsellors.
- ✓ CWWA counsellors are guided on how to create safe spaces for Aboriginal children and youth that support internalized oppression.

Fostering youth empowerment

- ✓ Aboriginal children and youth feel at ease with a CWWA counsellor who is able to support the diversity of Aboriginal experiences.
- ✓ Provides suggested activities for CWWA counsellors when working with Aboriginal students.
- ✓ VIP Manual outlines how can a CWWA counsellor approach diversity among Aboriginal students in the BC School system.

Developing and maintaining effective partnerships

- ✓ VIP Manual identifies key organizations that support First Nations Education.
- ✓ VIP Manual outlines how CWWA programs can build partnerships with First Nations schools and their communities.

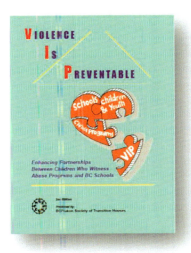

SECTION 4: RESEARCH AND EVALUATION

What are Indigenous methodologies in community research?[17]

Indigenous methodologies approach research from an Indigenous worldview that is holistic and includes the spirit, emotions, heart and body. Cultural protocols, values and behaviours are viewed as integral parts of methodology. They are seen as factors to be built into research and to be thought about and integrated openly as part of the design. Protocols, values and behaviours are discussed as part of the final results of a study and disseminated in culturally appropriate ways and in a language that can be understood by the community. Reporting back and sharing knowledge are two research components that are often not addressed in scientific research. In community based research, the community orientation and identity tends to influence the research approach.

What are some of the possibilities, challenges and responsibilities?

- Community participation and ownership at all levels of research process must be evident. Community control of the research process (see page 86 for discussion of ownership principles).

- Researchers who are doing research in Indigenous communities have a responsibility to know something about the history of Indigenous peoples. This history includes an awareness and understanding of the existence of Indigenous cultures, traditions, worldviews, and philosophies.

- Indigenous and non-Indigenous researchers who tackle research in Indigenous contexts must have a knowledge base and understanding of Western research methods as a mechanism of colonization. With this knowledge comes the responsibility to engage in research projects that empower, liberate and "Indigenize" rather than colonize, control, and oppress. Research then becomes an instrument of healing, restoration, recovery and power.

Suggested reading

Absolon, K. & Willett, C. (2004)
Aboriginal research: Berry picking and hunting in the 21st Century. First peoples Child & Family Review. 9(1), 5-17. Available online at www.fncfcs.com

Absolon, K., & Willett, C. (2005). Putting ourselves forward: Location in Aboriginal research methodology. In L. Brown & S. Strega (Eds.), Research as resistance: Critical, Indigenous and anti-oppressive research approaches. Toronto: Canadian Scholars Press.

Nabigon, H., Hagey, R., Webster, S., MacKay, R. (1998). The learning circle as a research method: The trickster and windigo in research. Native Social Work Journal, 2, 113-137.

Gilchrist, L. (1997). Aboriginal communities and social science research: Voyeurism in transition. Native Social Work Journal, 1, 69-85.

St. Denis, V. (1992). Community-based participatory research: Aspects of the concept relevant for practice. Native Studies Review, 8, 51-74.

Wilson, S. (2001). What is an Indigenous research methodology? Canadian Journal of Native Education, 25, 175-179.

---

[17] The authors wish to acknowledge Dr. Kathy Absolon of Wilfrid Laurier University for her assistance with this section. Dr. Absolon wrote the sections on Indigenous Methodologies, Research and Evaluation Considerations, The Building Blocks of an Evaluation, and Considerations for Interviewers (starting page 82).

WHAT ARE THE EXPECTATIONS OF RESEARCHERS?

Indigenous researchers are expected to have a knowledge set that is steeped in their own cultural history. They are also expected by their communities and by the institutions that employ them, to have some form of historical and critical analysis of the role of research in the Indigenous world and to be able to advance Indigenous knowledge, worldviews and methodologies in their research agenda. Indigenous researchers, in a sense, have dual knowledge sets and are expected to be functional and masters at both our own worldview and Euro-Western worldviews.

Non-Indigenous researchers are expected by the Indigenous community to have an understanding and appreciation for the impact of colonization and imperialism on the communities and their people. Non-Indigenous researchers are expected to develop a knowledge set that, recognizing Indigenous peoples' worldview, is critically conscious and can assist as an alley in advancing Indigenous peoples / communities agendas.

> *"Researchers have an obligation to de-mystify research for community partners and to help community partners understand how searching for knowledge and knowledge production is an everyday occurrence that we all do. Research is simply the act of acquiring information and knowledge. Too often in the past, research is something that has been done to participants with them receiving little or no benefit. De-mystifying research means being clear about the how, what and why of the search process. It also means including the community at every step in the re-search process."*
>
> Dr. Kathy Absolon
> Wilfrid Laurier University

Different approaches and methodologies that are being developed to ensure that research with Indigenous peoples can be more respectful, ethical, sympathetic and useful. Aboriginal research methodologies require Aboriginal paradigms so the community would expect the researcher to have some knowledge or be prepared to work with them to ensure Aboriginal paradigms guide the methodologies.

Researchers also need to be aware that some communities have developed their own ethics committees to deal with appropriation issues in research. These groups may be contacted as an additional source of support.

CONSIDERATIONS FOR RESEARCHERS – THE BIG PICTURE

For non-Aboriginal researchers venturing into the area of research with Aboriginal partners and youth, there will be many opportunities to apply research skills you have developed in your other work, but there will also be new challenges and opportunities. (Rethinking Research Priorities[18], Awareness of Specific Ethical Frameworks[19], and the Importance of Partnerships[20]).

Re-thinking Research Priorities: Conducting research with Aboriginal partners may require a shift in your worldview as a researcher. Your particular interests and mandates may need to be aligned with other priorities. The Coalition for Juvenile Justice (2000) recommends that research be designed around the principles of practicality and local relevance, community involvement, and cultural sensitivity.

The Importance of Partnerships: The history of research with Aboriginal people in Canada has been parallel to other areas in that it has been one of exploitation and domination. More recently, there has been a shift to engage in more collaborative ventures with researchers and communities as partners. The *Pimatisiwin* and *National Aboriginal Health Organization* journals have excellent articles on community-based research partnerships.

Awareness of Specific Ethical Frameworks: In beginning to develop Community-based Researcher Partnerships, it is important to be aware of the range of ethical issues that arise. There are a number of different helpful frameworks. We recommend the National Aboriginal Health Organization's *Considerations and Templates for Ethical Research Practices* as an excellent starting place.

Importance of documenting process: Some of the most important lessons that may arise from your research are in the challenges and successes of the research partnership. Documentation of these processes provides great assistance to others. The *Kahnawake Schools Diabetes Prevention Project (KSDPP)* has done an excellent job at this type of documentation, and published a number of excellent papers.

---

[18] Coalition for Juvenile Justice. (2000). Enlarging the healing circle: Ensuring justice for American Indian children. Washington, DC: Author.

[19] NAHO's *Considerations and Templates for Ethical Research Practices* is available online at
http://www.naho.ca/firstnations/english/documents/toolkits/FNC_ConsiderationsandTemplatesInformationResource.pdf

[20] See, for example, Salsberg et al., (2007). Knowledge, capacity, and readiness: translating successful experience in community-based participatory research for health promotion. Available at
http://www.pimatisiwin.com/Articles/5.2F_Knowledge_Capacity_and_Readiness.pdf

ADDITIONAL CONSIDERATIONS FOR RESEARCHERS

Research must benefit Aboriginal people as well as the researcher.	• Research conducted with Aboriginal people should make a positive difference in their communities. Researchers must ensure that the design, research questions, and the way the data are collected, interpreted, and communicated benefits Aboriginal people and does not harm them in any way. Research should be built upon the strengths of Aboriginal people and their communities.
Research must be culturally appropriate and relevant to the community.	• A researcher should understand and respect Aboriginal world views, and these should be incorporated into research questions and design to the extent possible. Researchers should learn about Indigenous Methodologies (see page 88-89 for overview).
The researcher has an obligation to learn about and apply Aboriginal cultural protocols that are relevant to the community involved in the research.	• Aboriginal communities are diverse in their languages, backgrounds, and traditions. Protocols can vary from group to group and from one community to the next. The research team needs to learn from the communities they are working with, and honour the differences among them in their research. For examples, issues that might arise include gift giving and signed consent.
Researchers should support the training and education of Aboriginal people to build community research capacity.	• Aboriginal people must be given the opportunity to learn about the role of research, the research process and be taught the skills to conduct research. Well trained Aboriginal researchers ideally should conduct Aboriginal research with their communities.
Research projects should be designed to allow continuous opportunities for consideration by the Aboriginal community.	• Research with Aboriginal communities should be flexible so that Aboriginal people or the wider community has the time to consider the proposed project and its components, and to discuss its implication before the project begins, but also at various stages throughout the project.

Engaging and Empowering Aboriginal Youth: A Toolkit for Service Providers

ETHICAL CONSIDERATIONS– OCAP PRINCIPLES

Although there are numerous frameworks and ethical standards with which researchers should be familiar, the OCAP principles are central to designing mutually beneficial research projects in conjunction with Aboriginal communities. The following description of the OCAP principles is taken from the document, *OCAP: Ownership, Control, Access and Possession*[21]. Although this document refers specifically to First Nations communities, the principles are applicable to all Aboriginal community-based research. The OCAP principles are defined as follows:

Ownership
- Refers to the relationship of a First Nations community to its cultural knowledge/data/information.
- The principle states that a community or group owns information collectively in the same way that an individual owns their personal information. It is distinct from stewardship [or possession].

Control
- The principle of control asserts that First Nations Peoples, their communities and representative bodies are within their rights in seeking to control all aspects of research and information management processes which impact them. First Nations control of research can include all stages of a particular research project – from conception to completion.
- The principle extends to the control of resources and review processes, the formulation of conceptual frameworks, data management and so on.

Access
- First Nations people must have access to information and data about themselves and their communities, regardless of where it is currently held.
- The principle also refers to the right of First Nations communities and organizations to manage and make decisions regarding access to their collective information. This may be achieved, in practice, through standardized, formal protocols.

Possession
- While ownership identifies the relationship between a people and their data in principle, possession or stewardship is more literal.
- Although not a condition of ownership per se, possession (of data) is a mechanism by which ownership can be asserted and protected. When data owned by one party is in the possession of another, there is a risk of breach or misuse. This is particularly important when trust is lacking between the owner and possessor.

OCAP principles need to be considered and integrated into every step of the research process. The National Aboriginal Health Organization document cited here provides specific and concrete strategies and examples of how to apply this principles and practice.

---

[21] First Nations Centre. (2007). *OCAP: Ownership, Control, Access and Possession*.
Available at: http://www.naho.ca/firstnations/english/documents/FNC-OCAP_001.pdf

RESEARCH AND EVALUATION CONSIDERATIONS

Research and evaluation are important components in the provision of services. First and foremost, we want to know that the programs we are offering meet the needs of the youth and are not resulting in negative unintended consequences.

Regardless of your own interest in research and evaluation, the current funding climate requires the collection and interpretation of data that support the effectiveness of the programs you are offering. Furthermore, most organizations now need to supplement any sources of core funding with community-based or corporate grants, and successfully attaining these grants typically requires the inclusion of an evaluation plan. For community organizations, large-scale, well-designed program evaluation studies with control groups are nearly impossible given their mandates and resources. Satisfaction surveys, exit surveys, and other participant feedback mechanisms serve as useful alternatives.

There are many different types of research. Research is generally qualitative and/or quantitative. Most qualitative research attempts to capture the experiences of subjects, whereas qualitative is more concerned with measurement. Wanting to determine the effectiveness or value of a program is called program evaluation and this type of research can be either quantitative or qualitative or a mixture of both. Program evaluation research requires an identified outcome, a means of collecting the requisite information, and a method of interpreting the information.

PROGRAM EVALUATION: MAKING YOUR EVALUATION A GOOD ONE!

An evaluation should be useful to the people who request the information, practical to implement, conducted in an ethical manner, and be accurate. There are three basic stages in the process, outlined below:

THE BUILDING BLOCKS OF AN EVALUATION

It is important to define your objectives and the results you expect. An objective is an identifiable action or activity that is to be completed in a specific time period. When a program has stated its objectives then an evaluation has something to work with as the design begins.

TYPES OF EVALUATION STUDIES:
There are three types of evaluation studies. These types differ in terms of the stage of a project at which they occur and the questions that they address.

Needs Assessment – answers questions about what kinds of problems, who has most urgent needs, what are community goals, etc.

Process Evaluation – conducted during a program to see how things are going and to see how it can be improved, made more effective, save money, serve more people, etc.

Impact Evaluation – done at the end of a program/project to find out the effectiveness on the community. It helps to determine whether or not the planned project occurred, the impact it has or had on those involved, whether it is worth continuing or expanding, and the costs.

EVALUATION STRATEGIES

Determining the types of questions to be asked is based on the expectations of the program and its objectives and goals. It is important to prioritize the evaluation needs. Strategies for data collection can involve a number of interview and circle processes as outlined below:

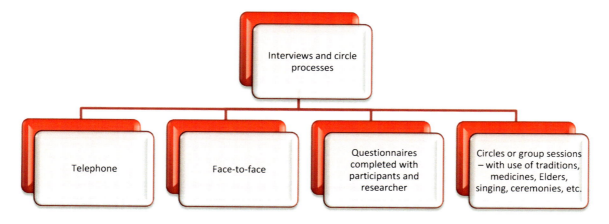

Interviews and circle processes

Telephone

Face-to-face

Questionnaires completed with participants and researcher

Circles or group sessions – with use of traditions, medicines, Elders, singing, ceremonies, etc.

IMPORTANT CONSIDERATIONS FOR INTERVIEWERS

There are a number of strategies for conducting effective interviews. The following list provides some of these guidelines:

- Interviewers should refrain from giving their opinions.
- If using written questions, "pilot test" the questions first to ensure they are clear.
- Check your language to see if the interviewee is comfortable.
- Keep the questions simple and clear.
- Interview one person at a time
- Don't start questions with a "why" – not always useful.
- Make sure to get consent.

TYPES OF QUESTIONS TO CONSIDER:

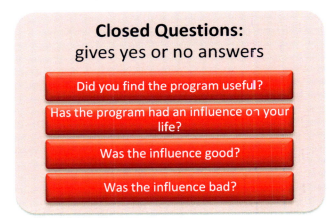

Closed Questions:
gives yes or no answers

- Did you find the program useful?
- Has the program had an influence on your life?
- Was the influence good?
- Was the influence bad?

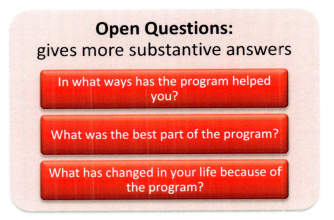

Open Questions:
gives more substantive answers

- In what ways has the program helped you?
- What was the best part of the program?
- What has changed in your life because of the program?

ATTENDING TO PROCESS

Researchers can ask themselves process questions and make notes on their thoughts during the evaluation. Examples of process questions include:

- Do the documents and files match what people are saying?
- Is there a positive feeling about the program?
- Can you describe the benefits that participants get from the program?
- Are those benefits written elsewhere (e.g., from interview, in existing files)
- What are the major strengths of the program?
- What are the major weaknesses of the program?

It is important to write these notes immediately while the "feel" is fresh in your mind.

Engaging and Empowering Youth through Research

Throughout this toolkit we have emphasized the importance of engaging and empowering youth and provided specific strategies to increase these outcomes. Engagement and empowerment of youth is also an important consideration in research and evaluation. Through involving youth in research, you are maintaining high ethical standards in terms of ownership of data, you increase the validity and relevance of the research, and you are supporting the development of interest and skills for tomorrow's researchers.

> *"Not only do youth 'find their voice' through participation in programs, but they also need to 'find their voice' in the research and design and delivery of evaluation mechanisms and in the dissemination of the results of evaluations."*
>
> *Dr. Marie Battiste*
> *Academic Director, Aboriginal Education Research Centre*

Considerations for Involving Youth in Research[22]

Research Activities

- Youth can be involved in developing research priorities and questions
- Youth can help carry out research activities, with proper preparation
- Youth can contribute to analysis of data, identifying conclusions and recommendation setting with researchers.

Dissemination

- Youth can assist with reporting and disseminating results
- It is important to think about how to return data to youth -- through provision of raw data, magazine articles, fact sheets, etc.
- Data need to be available to youth in a manner that they can access to inform their work (e.g., with youth councils, as social activists)
- Youth can be an effective voice for bringing forward recommendations to policy action groups.

---

[22] The authors acknowledge Dr. Marie Battiste's contribution to this section.

CHALLENGES IN IDENTIFYING THE IMPACT OF PREVENTION PROGRAMS

Another type of research is prevention research. This research is a form of evaluation research but focuses on establishing the *absence* of a negative outcome rather than the *presence* of a positive outcome. In reality, much prevention research does both. For example, a program evaluation might explore whether youth are more likely to use condoms during sexual intercourse (i.e., presence of a behaviour) in addition to whether they are more likely to delay onset of sexual intercourse (i.e., absence of behaviour).

There are a number of challenges involved with evaluating prevention programs:

Establishing Reasonable Outcomes	• Are we trying to prevent alcohol use or focusing more on other drugs? Are we trying to prevent binge drinking but acknowledging that some experimentation with alcohol may be normative? Are we trying to prevent unsafe decisions made while under the influence? • Appropriate outcomes will differ depending on the age of the youth, the challenges facing them, and the intensity of the intervention. Philosophical and political factors may also influence these decisions (i.e., whether or not a harm reduction approach is considered acceptable or whether the desired outcome is an all-or-nothing proposition).
Selecting a Timeframe	• What is the timeframe for the anticipated changes? Do we expect to see them immediately following the intervention or program? Do we expect them to show up later in development? • There are many documented research examples of both immediate effects and "sleeper effects" (i.e., impacts that only emerged in the context of longitudinal follow-up).
Measuring Problems versus Strengths	• If we are simultaneously trying to build youth assets and prevent harm, is one of those things more important to demonstrate? • How do you interpret findings that show the youth have better coping skills but are still engaging in bullying?

CHALLENGES IN CONDUCTING PREVENTION RESEARCH WITH ABORIGINAL YOUTH

Beyond the typical challenges of prevention research, there are other challenges that arise uniquely in working with Aboriginal youth, families, and communities:

Determining appropriate outcomes: The first challenge is to determine appropriate outcomes and whether they are culturally appropriate. For example, a program designed to increase coping skills may conceptualize coping from a Western European view focused on the development of action-oriented coping skills, which may or may not be appropriate for a particular group of Aboriginal youth. Similarly, a program teaching communication skills might emphasize the role of eye contact in assertive communication, but in many First Nations cultures eye contact is a more nuanced dynamic that may be appropriate in some situations but not in others. Without an appreciation of these differences, rating youth on particular outcomes might be misleading.

Inadequate culturally appropriate measures: The use of standardized measures generally aids in the interpretation and comparison of data; however, most measures have been designed for and normed with non-Aboriginal populations. In many cases they have been developed with a specific group with respect to education and SES, such as measures developed with and normed on university students. These measures may not be culturally sensitive in their format, or questions. Interpretation of the data is difficult due to lack of comparable norms.

Challenges in Prevention Research with Aboriginal Youth

Infeasibility of the control group design: Control groups play an important role in research with youth because of the developmental changes taking place. For example, school connectedness typically decreases over the course of Grade 9. Thus, an evaluation that compares students' scores pre- and post- involvement with a school-based initiative to improve students' connection to school might find that the program was ineffective (because scores either stayed the same or dropped slightly). However, school connectedness dropped *less* for students in the program than it would have otherwise, in which case the program had a positive impact. With programming that is embedded in the school and community, it is very challenging to determine an appropriate control group. It is also ethically questionable to withhold programming that youth are reporting to find helpful in order to establish an appropriate control group.

Difficulty capturing systemic changes: The most straightforward evaluation focuses solely on the youth involved with the services. However, according to our guiding principles, these efforts need to be embedded in partnerships with families and communities. As a result, it is likely that there will be changes at the family and community levels that also need to be captured. Other systems involved with the programming – such as the educational system – may also experience changes that should be captured as part of the evaluation. In the best case scenario, documentation of positive changes in other systems will strengthen the sustainability and funding prospects for your initiatives. In other cases, assessing the larger system will alert you to possible negative unforeseen impacts.

On the following pages a number of practical and specific strategies are offered for program evaluation and prevention research.

EVALUATION STRATEGY #1: BE REALISTIC ABOUT THE CHANGES YOU EXPECT TO SEE AND THE TIMEFRAMES IN WHICH YOU EXPECT TO SEE THEM

One of the significant requirements facing organizations who receive external funding for doing community-based research is the need to demonstrate that the program or service resulted in some positive change in participant knowledge, attitudes, and behaviours. Often grant applications or funders will suggest certain outcomes of interest and timeframes in which they would like to see change. Often the timeframes are not very feasible -- long-lasting behavioural change and personal growth take time!

Organizations (and funders) need to be realistic about the changes you can expect to see within the timeframes you are given. It is important to resist identifying the changes you think your funders want to see, if the goals are unrealistic, as you are setting yourself up for failure.

For example – a new anti-bullying program is being implemented in a school. The funding was announced in September, the program will be fully implemented by December, and the final report is due to the funder in July.

Unrealistic outcomes

More realistic early markers of success could include:

- Significant reductions in bullying (in light of the short timeframe).
- Significantly higher scores on academic measures.
- Reductions in drop-out rates.
- Clear demonstration of skills acquisition among youth.

- Increased participation of parents or youth in activities.
- Getting all school staff trained in the program.
- Ability to get a program running in the school.
- Stakeholder satisfaction.
- Regular meetings for a multi-stakeholder advisory group.
- The formation of an anti-bullying youth committee.
- Development of a manual or document outlining your successes and challenges in project development and implementation.

EVALUATION STRATEGY #2: ACCESS ABORIGINAL JOURNALS WRITTEN IN THE CANADIAN CONTEXT FOR IDEAS ABOUT MEASURES AND METHODOLOGY

There are some excellent journals available online that focus on issues facing Aboriginal youth and communities in Canada. Articles in these journals provide good examples of appropriate measurement strategies, ethical considerations, and other related research topics. We recommend:

* **Journal of Aboriginal Health (at http://www.naho.ca/english/journal/php)**

This journal is published by the National Aboriginal Health Organization. In addition to the journal, they have excellent publications (e.g., Understanding Health Indicators) available on their website. The Journal of Aboriginal Health is dedicated exclusively to Aboriginal health issues in Canada. Published by the National Aboriginal Health Organization (NAHO), the journal was established with the intention of fostering a dynamic community of people concerned with issues of Aboriginal health.

Journal of Aboriginal Health
Journal de la santé autochtone

* **First Nations Child & Family Review (at http://www.fncfcs.org/pubs/onlineJournal.html)**

Published by the First Nations Child and Family Caring Society of Canada, this journal focuses on innovation and best practices in Aboriginal child welfare administration, research, policy and practice. The purpose of the First Peoples Child & Family Review is to "reach beyond the walls of academia" to promote child welfare research, practice, policy and education from a First Nations/Aboriginal perspective and to advance innovative approaches within the field of First Nations and Aboriginal child welfare.

FIRST NATIONS CHILD & FAMILY CARING SOCIETY OF CANADA

* Pimatisiwin: A Journal of Indigenous and Aboriginal Community Health (at http://www.pimatisiwin.com)

The goal of the Pimatisiwin Journal is to promote the sharing of knowledge and research experience between researchers, health professionals, and Aboriginal leaders and community members. The journal provides a forum for this diverse population to publish on research process and findings in a cross-disciplinary, cross-cultural setting. The primary focus is on health and health research in Indigenous communities. Articles can be of interest to many fields, including sociological, psychological, medical, anthropological, experiential, and methodological, both qualitative and quantitative in nature.

PIMATISIWIN
A Journal of Indigenous and Aboriginal Community Health

Existing measures do not need to abandored, rather, they need to be used judiciously. In some cases, modifications may be necessary and in other cases perhaps only parts of a measure are suitable. Furthermore, due to issues of assimilation and loss of culture, it is not appropriate to assume that a more culturally-relevant measure will make sense to all Aboriginal youth any more than it is appropriate to use a mainstream measure. Standardized measures do have the advantage of producing scores and numbers, which may be a useful adjunct to other types of information collected in an evaluation. Quantitative data can provide a compelling case to types of funders and policy makers who may be unconvinced by qualitative data alone. If you are undertaking scale development, it is important to undertake this process with direct input from youth and other community members. In selecting and using quantitative measures for evaluation, you may wish to consider the following:

Are there measures that have been successfully used with this population?

- Look at the measures other evaluators and researchers have used to measure similar outcomes. For example, the Aboriginal Youth Resiliency Studies is an ongoing initiative to measure resilience among Aboriginal youth For methodology and measures see Andersson, N., & Ledogar, R. J. (2008). The CIET Abcriginal Youth Resilience Studies: 14 years of capacity building and methods development in Canada. *Pimatisiwin: A Journal of Aboriginal and Indigenous Community Health, 6,* 65-88.

What measures have been adapted for use with this population?

- In some cases, widely used measures have been applied with a range of cultural groups and may have appropriate norms or modifications. For example, the widely used Self-Perception Profile for Adolescents has been adapted for use with Aboriginal youth by changing the comparative nature of the questionnaire (where youth are asked to say who of two hypothetical individuals they are more like) to use a scale format, because of the lack of comfort with comparing oneself to others among some Aboriginal groups.

Can you conduct focus groups to review your proposed data collection strategy?

- It is better to identify possible problems with your questionnaires before you have administered them widely, and having a few focus groups to review items and identify possible sources of misunderstanding can go a long way in this regard.

Can you corroborate the quantitative data you with qualitative data?

- In the end, you will feel most confident about using and interpreting quantitative data when these can be combined with qualitative data as well. Alternatively, you can hold more focus groups with stakeholders to help you interpret your quantitative data.

EVALUATION STRATEGY #4: COLLECT DATA FROM PARTNERS IN A SYSTEMATIC MANNER

Using multiple informants when collecting data can capture successes *and* challenges from a variety of perspectives. Parents, community partners, teachers, administrators, and program developers can complete surveys or participate in focus groups and feedback sessions to provide their input and perspectives. These stakeholders can be important sources of information about the program and the perceived benefits to youth.

Example 1: General Feedback about Program and Impact

The following example is a questionnaire used with partner community organizations to evaluate the *TERF* program at New Directions:

---

1. Please indicate how much you agree with each of the statements below using the following scale:

1	2	3	4	5
Strongly Disagree	*Disagree*	*Neither agree nor disagree*	*Agree*	*Strongly agree*

   a. There is a cooperative relationship between my agency and TERF.
   b. I get feedback about participants in a timely manner.
   c. TERF offers a wide range of services.
   d. TERF services are high quality.
   e. I will continue to work with TERF.

For the following 5 questions respondents answer yes/no/don't know and provide comments:
1. Has the program improved the physical health of the participants?
2. Has the program improved the emotional wellbeing of the participants?
3. Has the program improved the spiritual wellbeing of the participants?
4. Has the program changed the attitudes of the participants?
5. Has the program changed the behaviour of the participants?

Open-ended questions:
6. What is the overall value of the program to participants? The community?
7. What are the TERF programs strengths?
8. What are some of the problems with the program?
9. How do you think services could be improved?

Example 2: Partner Input about a Specific Issue

Data from partners can also be collected to examine a particular issue or to answer a specific research question. The following example was used by the *Uniting Our Nations* research team at the Fourth R to study youth engagement factors among participants. Youth were interviewed directly about their engagement process, but this questionnaire was used to assess adult perceptions.

Instructions:

The purpose of this research questionnaire is to identify youth engagement factors related to initiatives that adapt violence prevention programs for use with First Nations youth. Engagement refers to the meaningful participation and sustained involvement of individuals in activities (Centre for Excellence in Youth Engagement, 2003). The questions below ask for your opinion about factors that led First Nations youth to be engaged in the first Uniting our Nations video (April 2005), the summer Curriculum project (July 2006), and the second video project (October 2005).

The process of youth engagement can be understood in terms of initiating and sustaining factors, and challenges encountered.

- *Initiating Factors* refers to how and why youth become involved in projects.
- *Sustaining Factors* refers to factors that maintain youth involvement or commitment to a project.
- *Challenges or barriers* to participating in the project include factors that may prevent or inhibit youth from becoming involved or staying involved in the project.
- Initiating, sustaining, and challenging factors can be at the individual, organizational/social, and community levels

Please note that all responses to this questionnaire will be kept confidential. You are not required to indicate your name, school, or organization when completing this questionnaire

Please check one.

- ⭘ I am an Administrator
- ⭘ a First Nations counsellor
- ⭘ a Facilitator
- ⭘ Research/Project staff

1. **INTIATING FACTORS:** What were some individual (e.g. incentives), organizational/school (e.g. being approached by a counsellor they know), or community (e.g. project located at The University of Western Ontario) factors that led students to be initially involved in the project?
2. **SUSTAINING FACTORS:** What were some individual, organizational/school, or community factors that maintained student commitment to these projects?
3. **CHALLENGES OR BARRIERS:** If applicable, identify any individual, organizational/school, or community-level challenges that were encountered related to students becoming involved and or staying involved in the project? What are some solutions to these challenges?
4. If applicable, please identify any other challenges encountered during the project.
5. What recommendations do you have to engage youth in future projects?
6. Please add any additional comments you have about the projects.

EVALUATION STRATEGY #5: MEASURE PROCESS NOT JUST OUTCOMES

Often we design evaluations to measure longer range outcomes such as self-esteem, self-efficacy, and behavior. While these outcomes are important, it is equally important to measure the participants' perceptions of the program, particularly in respect to the guiding principles outlined in this toolkit. These data will provide important feedback about the successes and challenges of your program, as well as possible areas for improvement.

The following two surveys are used by the *TERF* program at New Directions. Together, they provide valuable feedback on cultural identity, youth engagement, and youth empowerment. The first addresses youth's comfort with the program staff (which is a critical issue for engaging high risk and alienated youth) and also the extent to which the program addresses cultural identity. It was adapted from one developed by the Child Welfare League of America.

Survey 1

Please indicate whether you agree with the following statement or not, as indicated by the following scale:

1	2	3	4	5
Strongly Disagree	*Disagree*	*Neither agree nor disagree*	*Agree*	*Strongly agree*

a)   I was welcomed and made to feel comfortable when I arrived at this program

b)   I was spoken to in my first language

c)   I was spoken to in a kind and gentle manner

d)   I feel comfortable with the staff in this program

e)   I believe this program is interested in me and my family's problems

f)   I get along with the staff in this program

g)   I find the staff helpful

h)   I believe the program staff understand my problems

i)   I feel the staff who take care of me are sincere and treat me fairly

j)   I believe the staff are interested in me and my family's cultural background

k)   The program staff show respect for me

l)   I believe the staff who work with me try to provide good service to all the people in this program

m) There are several staff who are of my race / ethnic background

n)   In this program I have people I can talk to about my cultural identity

o)   I am receiving culturally appropriate supports and services

p)   It is important to me that there be a cultural aspect to this program

q)   I am comfortable and satisfied with how this program is going for me

r)   I am satisfied with the program

s)   I would recommend this program to other young women like myself

---

The second survey addresses youth empowerment with respect to healthier relationships, lifestyle choices, goal setting, and academic performance. It was designed specific to a particular program. The use of rated items facilitates the pooling of data from a number of youth, while the open-ended questions provide an opportunity for more detailed and individual-level input.

Survey 2

Please indicate whether you agree with the following statement or not, as indicated by the following scale:

1	2	3	4	5
Strongly Disagree	Disagree	Neither agree nor disagree	Agree	Strongly agree

a) Since I started this program I am learning to think about goals for myself

b) I feel I am already starting to achieve some of my goals

c) I feel I have changed since I came here

d) The program has reduced my use of alcohol and / or marijuana

e) The program has reduced my use of hard drugs like cocaine and amphetamines

f) My school performance has improved since being in the program

g) I have a more positive attitude about being in school since being in the program

h) I have used thing I learned in the program in my everyday life

i) I am more confident since being in the program

j) I am more hopeful and positive about my future since being in the program

k) I feel I have more control over my life since being in the program

l) I feel better about myself since being in the program

m) I feel more independent since being in the program

n) I feel less alone since being in the program

o) I am making healthier choices for myself since being in the program

p) I have healthier relationships with other since being in the program

q) I am more satisfied with my relationships with others since being in the program

r) My life is better now than before I came to the program

In addition, there are several open-ended questions about changes in physical, emotional, and spiritual well-being, attitude, and perceptions of the program.

EVALUATION STRATEGY #6: CONSIDER FOCUS GROUPS AS A SOURCE OF DATA

Focus groups offer a number of advantages compared to surveys or individual interviews. They do not have the same reading comprehension demands as surveys. Similar to individual interviews you are able to follow up on specific answers and get more detail, but the group format makes it a more efficient process. Youth may be more comfortable answering questions in a group than one-on-one.

There are a number of considerations in planning focus groups to maximize effectiveness:

A written plan is important – it can either include many specific questions or be more of a content guide from which questions are developed during the process (see next page).	It is important to emphasize that a focus group is not a consensus driven process and that you are looking for areas where people have different perspectives.	Information needs to be recorded as closely as possible in the participants own words. Facilitators may consider the use of a designated note taker or audio record the session.
It is not advisable to use a pre-existing therapy group as a focus group because of the norms and dynamics that have developed during the therapeutic process.	Focus groups with Aboriginal youth can be adapted to a sharing circle format as youth may be familiar and comfortable with the concept. Each youth is given a chance to comment on a particular question or issue in turn, while also knowing that they can pass.	

It is helpful to have written instructions to guide the facilitators. For example, it is important to explain confidentiality to participants. Here is a sample script used at New Directions:

The staff at TRY is dedicated to making your experience here as helpful as possible. We are from New Directions but not from this program and we have come to ask for your input about TRY. New Directions has asked us, people from outside the program, in hopes that you will feel more comfortable telling us your honest opinion.

We are going to ask for your opinion on issues related to this program and we want you to know that although we will be letting the staff know all your overall opinions, we will not tell them who said what. That will be confidential. If, however, any of you disclose that you've been abused or harassed or if any of you make threats to harm someone else we will not keep that confidential and will need to tell this to a Senior Manager at New Directions.

We are not experts on this program, so if anything seems unclear we will be asking you to tell us more about your program as we go along.

In addition to providing clear instructions prior to beginning the focus group, it is important to offer some sort of debriefing at the end. At the very least, participants need to know whom they could contact if they are uncomfortable or dissatisfied with the process. For example:

> *Finish by thanking them and letting them know that if they have felt uncomfortable talking about their concerns in this focus group but have something they would like to discuss, please remind them of the suggestion box or tell them they can call you – [give extension]. You can also remind them that their Bill of Rights encourages them to call the Executive Director.*

Sample Focus Group Template

Topic	Key Points	Sample Questions
General	– Overall experience in program – Like – Helpful – Dislike – Obstacles	How do you feel, overall, about your experiences in [name of program]? 1. Liked and was helpful? 2. More specifically, what did you like about the program? 3. What was particularly helpful in the program? 4. Disliked and made it hard? 5. Were you dissatisfied or uncomfortable with anything that happened during your participation in the program? 6. Did anything make it hard for you to engage or come to the program?
Benefits from the program	– Benefits from program – Changes in: ✓ Knowledge ✓ Skills ✓ Behaviour	1. What did you get out of coming to the program? 2. How have you changed since you came to the program? OR What has changed in the things you know or you do since you came to the program?
Expectations about the program	– Initial expectations – Future expectations: ✓ Keep the same ✓ Change	1. What did you hope to get out of the program when you first came? 2. What did you think the program was about? 3. What do you want to make certain remains the same? 4. What do you think should change? OR What are you not getting out of the program that you think the program should be providing?
Culture	– Awareness of culture – Feelings about exposure to culture	1. How has the program increased your awareness of your own culture or other cultures? 2. Has this contact with culture been a good experience or a bad experience?
Other	– Additional comments	1. Do you have any additional comments?

EVALUATION STRATEGY #7: USE EXISTING DATA TO DOCUMENT THE IMPACT OF YOUR PROGRAM

For some programs, there may be existing data that can be accessed to document successes or to show impact. In some cases, these existing data can be used to estimate financial impact or impact on other systems (such as the justice system). These types of comparisons may be particularly powerful with funders and policy makers.

Example # 1

In external evaluation conducted on the TERF program, the researchers from RESOLVE Manitoba (Research and Education to Solutions of Violence and Abuse) were able to use numerous existing estimates to document the impacts of the program. For example, by utilizing existing estimate of the cost to society per exploited individual, they were able to demonstrate that assisting 15 to 20 individuals to exit the sex trade every year translates to a savings of millions of dollars. Comparison of incarceration costs versus program costs are provided to show the cost efficiency of the program. They also provide rates of return to school and gainful employment, to help bolster the financial argument for providing services. These markers do not take the place of the other important outcomes provided in terms of personal satisfaction, safety and growth, but they provide a more comprehensive picture.

Example # 2

In looking at the impact of the pilot implementation of the *First Nations Cultural Leadership Course,* program developers examined the students' grades and number of absences for each of their courses. This simple comparison demonstrated that students' marks in the course were much higher than in their other courses, and that on average, they had 25% fewer absents for the class. Such findings do not constitute an evaluation of the program, but provided one more piece of data about the engagement strategies being used. This example also highlights the importance of partnerships, as it is through a partnership with the school board that these data were accessed.

One of the problems is that in many cases there are not data specific to Aboriginal youth. In some cases, data tracking is improving in general. For example, many school boards are now implementing Aboriginal voluntary self-identification programs that will allow them to congregate data they are already collecting to look at these youth distinctly. This type of policy will mean that data for anything the school board collects (such as literacy scores, demographic information) can be extracted for Aboriginal youth. Better group data will provide useful benchmarks in looking at the impact of different initiatives both structurally (does adding more First Nations Counsellors increase graduation rates in a school) and individually (does involvement in a peer mentoring program increase graduation rates)?

TOOLKIT SUMMARY

Much of what we have learned from others about working with Aboriginal youth and partners has been passed to us through conversations and relationships. This toolkit represents an attempt to document some of those lessons and provide a compendium of ideas, strategies and resources for those undertaking similar work. We have tried to find a balance between presenting organizing concepts and practical strategies as we think both are critical. Working with Aboriginal youth in a respectful and appropriate way requires a high degree of self-awareness regarding *why* you make the choices you do.

We believe the principles we have used to organize this toolkit -- understanding and integrating cultural identity, increasing youth engagement, fostering youth empowerment and developing and maintaining effective partnerships -- are foundational in this work. Without attending to these basics, programs may continue to experience setbacks, not reach their potential, or even do more harm than good. We recognize that operationalizing these principles is easier said than done, but believe that awareness of the importance of these principles is an important first step. If everyone in an organization is on the same page with respect to the importance of these principles, then progress will be made, a step at a time.

The information, strategies, and case studies represented in this toolkit grew out of input and guidance from a large number of individuals. Writing the toolkit has been a highly rewarding and educational process for the authors because of the generosity of these individuals in sharing their knowledge. At the same time, we know that there are many, many others out there who are doing innovative work with Aboriginal youth whose ideas are not represented in this document. It is our hope that people will contact us with their feedback and ideas, and that we will be able to integrate those additional perspectives into a revised version of this resource in a few years time. Anyone who wishes to contribute in this way can email their ideas to Claire Crooks at ccrooks@uwo.ca.

Finally, writing this toolkit was an incredible process for the authors as we learned more about the amazing work being done around the country. While some of the ideas presented in here were accessed through print or web sources, most of them came out of conversations with contributors and reviewers. Throughout this process we were moved by the commitment, creativity, and integrity of those working with youth. We were also inspired by the feedback of our youth reviewers. Their ideas and energy bode well for the changes already taking place to accelerate in the coming years. In the end, we believe it is the empowerment of these youth voices that will bring true and lasting change for Aboriginal youth, to the benefit of all Canadians.

REFERENCES

Absolon, K. & Willett, C. (2004). *Aboriginal research: Berry picking and hunting in the 21st Century.* First peoples Child & Family Review. 9(1), 5-17. Available online at: www.fncfcs.com.

Absolon, K., & Willett, C. (2005). Putting ourselves forward: Location in Aboriginal research methodology. In L. Brown & S. Strega (Eds.), Research as resistance: Critical, Indigenous and anti-oppressive research approaches. Toronto: Canadian Scholars Press.

Alderman, J., Balla, S., Blackstock, C., & Khanna, N. (2006). The Declaration of Accountability On The Ethical Engagement of Young People and Adults in Canadian Organizations. Ottawa, ON: First Nations Child and Family Caring Society of Canada. Available online at http://www.fncfcs.org/docs/declaration_accountability.pdf

Banks, James (2003). Levels of Multicultural Content: A Brief Summary. Available online at: http://resources.css.edu/DiversityServices/docs/LevelsofIntegrationofMulticulturalContent.pdf.

Centre of Excellence on Youth Engagement, Adult Allies in Action. Available online at: http://www.engagementcentre.ca/files/alliesFINAL_e_web.pdf.

Coalition for Juvenile Justice. (2000). Enlarging the healing circle: Ensuring justice for American Indian children. Washington, DC.

Community Education Unit, Children's Services and Programs Branch (2004). *Toward School plus Empowering High Schools as Communities of Learning and Support.* Available online at: http://www.sasked.gov.sk.ca/branches/pol_eval/community_ed/docs/hs2004splus.pdf

First Nations Centre. (2007). OCAP: Ownership, Control, Access and Possession. Available online at: http://www.naho.ca/firstnations/english/documents/FNC-OCAP_001.pdf.

First Nations Child & Family Caring Society of Canada (2003). Caring Across Boundaries. Available online at: http://www.fncfcs.com/projects/docs/CABInformationSheet.pdf.

Formsma, J. (2002). First Steps in Youth Engagement. Unpublished document.

Gilchrist, L. (1997). Aboriginal communities and social science research: Voyeurism in transition. Native Social Work Journal, 1, 69-85.

Klinck, J., Cardinal, C., Edwards, K., Gibson, N., Bisanz, J., & da Costa, J. (2005). Mentoring programs for Aboriginal youth. Pimatisiwin: A Journal of Aboriginal and Indigenous Community Health, 3, 109-130. Available online at www.pimatisiwin.com.

Nabigon, H., Hagey, R., Webster, S., & MacKay, R. (1998). *The learning circle as a research method: The trickster and windigo in research.* Native Social Work Journal, 2, 113-137.

National Aboriginal Health Office. *Considerations and Templates for Ethical Research Practices.* Available online at: http://www.naho.ca/firstnations/english/documents/toolkits/FNC_ConsiderationsandTemplatesInformationResource.pdf.

National Aboriginal Health Office. *Guidelines from the National Aboriginal Health Organization.* Available online at: http://www.naho.ca/english/documents/InterviewingElders--FINAL.pdf.

Ontario Ministry of Education and Training. *Integrating Aboriginal Teaching and Values into the Classroom.* Available online at: http://www.edu.gov.on.ca/eng/literacynumeracy/inspire/research/Toulouse.pdf.

Pridemore, W. A. (2004). Review of the Literature on Risk and Protective Factors of Offending Among Native Americans. Journal of Ethnicity in Criminal Justice, 2(4), 45-63.

R.A. Malatest and Associates, Ltd. Parent anc Education Engagement Partnership Project: A discussion paper. July 30, 2002. Available at http://www.bced.gov.bc.ca/abed/reports/parent_engage.pdf.

Saskatchewan Ministry of Education. *Empowering High Schools as Communities of Learning and Support.* Available online at: http://www.sasked.gov.sk.ca/branches/pol_eval/community_ed/docs/hs2004splus.pdf

Salsberg et al., (2007). Knowledge, capacity, and readiness: translating successful experience in community-based participatory research for health promotion. Available online at: http://www.pimatisiwin.com/Articles/5.2F_Knowledge_Capacity_and_Readiness.pdf.

St. Denis, V. (1992). *Community-based participatory research: Aspects of the concept relevant for practice.* Native Studies Review, 8, 51-74.

Ursel, E.J, Proulx, J., Dean, L., & S. Costello (2007). Evaluation of the TERF Youth and Adult Programs. Winnipeg, MB: RESOLVE. Available online at http://www.umanitoba.ca/resolve/publications/FINAL%20Evaluation%20of%20TERF%20Youth%20&%20Adult%20Program%20Report%202007.pdf.

White, J. and Jodoin, N. (2007). Aboriginal youth: A manual of promising suicide prevention strategies. Calgary, AB: Centre for Suicide Prevention. Available online at www.suicideinfo.ca/csp/assets/promstrat_manual.pdf.

Wilson, S. (2001). *What is an Indigenous research methodology?* Canadian Journal of Native Education, 25, 175-179.

Wolfe, D. A., Jaffe, P.G., & Crooks, C. V. (2006). *Adolescent risk behaviors: Why teens experiment and strategies to keep them safe.* New Haven, CT: Yale University Press.